Integrated Intellectual Asset Management

Integrated Intellectual Asset Management

A Guide to Exploiting and Protecting your Organization's Intellectual Assets

STEVE MANTON

GOWER

Published by
Gower Publishing Limited
Gower House
Croft Road
Aldershot
Hampshire GU11 3HR
England

Gower Publishing Company
Suite 420
101 Cherry Street
Burlington, VT 05401-4405
USA

Steve Manton has asserted his moral right under the Copyright, Designs and Patents Act, 1988, to be identified as the author of this work.

British Library Cataloguing in Publication Data
Manton, Steve
   Integrated intellectual asset management: a guide to
   exploiting and protecting your organization's intellectual
   assets
   1. Knowledge management
   I. Title
   658.4'038

ISBN: 0 566 08721 9

Library of Congress Cataloging-in-Publication Data
Manton, Steve.
  Integrated intellectual asset management: a guide to exploiting and protecting your
  organization's intellectual assets / by Steve Manton.
     p. cm.
  ISBN 0-566-08721-9
  1. Intellectual capital--Management. I. Title.

HD53.M36 2005
658.4'038--dc22

2005024898

Printed and bound in Great Britain by TJ International Ltd, Padstow, Cornwall

CONTENTS

LIST OF FIGURES

FOREWORD

This book is not short on ambition; it seeks to unify the management of knowledge and intellectual property, by providing a framework that will enable organizations to integrate the management of all intellectual assets into their existing business processes and practices.

The methods and tools underpinning this integrated approach to intellectual asset management (IAM) evolved over a number of years. However, the basic concepts can be illustrated using a case study, in which an intellectual asset plan was prepared to assist in the development of a large waste treatment plant. At the time of this review the plant's outline design had been completed and detailed engineering drawings were in preparation.

The generation of an intellectual asset plan follows a fairly standard process, involving one, or more, workshops convened to:

- identify the project, service or product's key intellectual assets (for example: know-how, data, software, and so on);
- identify those intellectual assets regarded as commercially sensitive, and the actions necessary to prevent unauthorized third party use (for example: patenting, secrecy, and so on);
- identify any threats to business-critical intellectual assets (for example: loss of key staff, blocking third party patents, and so on) and any actions necessary to quantify or mitigate risks;
- identify any actions that should be taken to exchange knowledge within, or outside, of the organization.

During the course of this review it became clear that:

- While many features of the design were potentially patentable, and a business case existed for the associated expenditure, such protection had not been sought. Further, because the project was perceived as innovative and ground-breaking by senior management it had been used as a show-case, with a number of potential customers given detailed information on these inventions.
- Many of these design features clearly had application across the organization. However, although well developed, these had not been shared with other internal projects – even though an organization-wide database had been established for sharing reports, and further a capability manual existed intended to capture and disseminate designs of this type.
- In general the project's most valuable "asset" was judged to be the close working relationship established with its customer, with this relationship likely to be critical in winning follow-up work. Unfortunately, a range of sub-contractors had been used on the project, and these had not only been given access to all aspects of the design, but they had also been allowed to develop their own contacts with the customer. It was clear that the project had not been given any guidance on which capabilities the organization as a whole regarded as commercially sensitive, and hence where contractors should, and should not, be used.
- The business process used to approve and manage the project had demanded that the project submit an intellectual property plan – but neither the project manager, nor those sanctioning the project, knew what such a document should contain; further, neither held any formal accountability to ensure a fit-for-purpose plan was developed and followed.

Ultimately, the blame for these mistakes mainly lay outside of the project:

- No strategic guidance had been provided to help the project identify those intellectual assets it could share, and those it needed to protect.
- The organization's system of accountabilities did not define responsibilities for the management of its intellectual assets.
- Training was inadequate and neither the project manager, nor those sanctioning the project, knew enough about intellectual assets to identify challenges and key actions.
- The organization's knowledge management systems were clumsy and inefficient, with their use neither encouraged nor incentivized.

- The poor quality of the organization's intellectual asset management was invisible to senior management and the Board.

In conclusion, intellectual asset management was not properly addressed within the organization's existing policy, strategy, accountabilities and management processes. However, outside of the intellectual asset arena its management framework was sound; a clear accountability framework existed, systems were in place to check the robustness of the project's business plans, the quality of the services provided to customers was routinely monitored, the technical competency of staff was checked, and so on. All these systems could, and should, have been extended to address intellectual assets, but for some reason these critical assets were being ignored.

Steve Manton
Managing Director
Intellectual Property and Asset Management
stevemanton@ip-am.co.uk

CHAPTER 1

INTRODUCTION

Whether you define documents, designs, know-how, software, data, patents and trademarks as intellectual property (IP) or more accurately as intellectual assets (IAs) the commercial success of most organizations will depend on their exploitation and protection. These assets may be called upon to fill a variety of roles including: reducing competitive pressures, helping to control the supply chain, generating license income and improving productivity.

It is therefore clear that both the quality, and commercial success, of an organization's products and services will depend on how well these underpinning intellectual assets are being managed. Despite this dependency most organizations seek to manage their intellectual assets using a range of stand-alone business processes that are, to a lesser or greater extent, divorced from the processes they use to manage their products and services.

Organizations using these "bolt on" business processes cannot hope to align their intellectual asset portfolio to business strategy. In practice, an organization can only succeed in developing, protecting and exploiting its intellectual assets when their management is fully integrated into existing business processes and culture. Similarly, if the responsibilities for managing the different forms of intellectual asset are fragmented then an organization will inevitably fail to take full advantage of its intellectual asset portfolio. A fully integrated approach to intellectual asset management (IAM) is required, focusing on the six areas shown in Figure 1.1 and discussed overleaf.

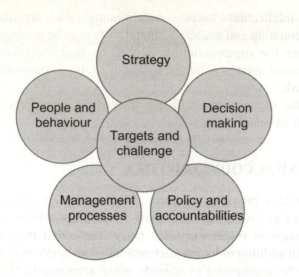

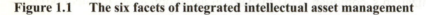

Figure 1.1   The six facets of integrated intellectual asset management

DECISION MAKING

Existing decision-making bodies and systems (such as project approval and bid-no-bid tools) should receive information on, and take due account of, both the sufficiency of the available intellectual assets and the quality of their management. The submission of this information, in the form of an intellectual asset plan, should be mandated in exactly the same way as is the case with financial data. If the preparation of fit-for-purpose intellectual asset plans is not the accepted norm within an organization, then decision-making systems may need formalised inputs; whereby strong guidance is given on the information any submission should contain. Further, the organization's system of accountabilities should define responsibilities for preparing, challenging and implementing these plans.

STRATEGY

A top-level intellectual asset strategy should define the role of intellectual assets in the organization and, in so doing, both assist in their management and guide decision making. Such an intellectual asset strategy should therefore address issues such as:

- how intellectual assets underpinning the organization's key differentiating and enabling capabilities are to be managed;
- whether the organization will seek to generate revenue from its intellectual assets via licensing, and if so, how opportunities are to be realized;
- how the organization will use trademarks to protect, develop and exploit its brand.

POLICY AND ACCOUNTABILITIES

Whereas strategy provides guidance to help decision makers, policy can be thought of as providing constraints by defining actions that are either mandated (such as respecting third party intellectual property rights) or prohibited. In addition to listing such actions in an intellectual asset strategy, it may also be appropriate to identify those accountable for ensuring the organization's compliance. However, in developing an intellectual asset policy, care must be taken to strike the right balance between management freedom and mandated policy.

PEOPLE AND BEHAVIOUR

Intellectual asset management should concern and involve almost everyone in an organization. Unfortunately, in most organizations, intellectual asset management is perceived as a task that can, and should, be delegated to a stand-alone function. Changing this perception, and creating an educated workforce, is often the rate determining factor when seeking to improve intellectual asset management. Any drive to improve awareness must not only have visible top-management support, but also be supported by a mixture of initiatives including: training programmes, highlighted examples of good practice, and the inclusion of intellectual asset skills within both job descriptions and the organization's competency framework.

TARGETS AND CHALLENGE

To help strengthen intellectual asset management senior management, or the corporate body, should routinely challenge both how effectively intellectual assets are being managed by the operational businesses, and the health of the intellectual asset portfolio. This should involve the use of both key performance indicators (KPIs), and metrics capable of showing the health of the intellectual asset portfolio, so that targets can be set and trends monitored.

MANAGEMENT PROCESSES

In addition to those described above organizations will use a vast range of detailed processes designed to manage their knowledge, information, patents, trademarks, and so on. These range from processes designed to ensure know-how is shared, to the way in which the costs associated with filing patents and trademarks are recovered. It is clear that these detailed processes must operate seamlessly with, and provide support to, the other facets of intellectual asset management as described here.

CHAPTER 2

BACKGROUND

DEFINITIONS

The term **intellectual property** (IP) is used to describe a range of intellectual assets including documentation, drawings, databases, software, procedures, patents and trademarks.

Intellectual property rights (IPRs) are rights, granted by the State, restricting unauthorized use of intellectual property. Some IPRs are granted automatically; whilst some must be won, and maintained, by an often expensive legal process. These are described more fully in Appendix 1.

The term **intellectual asset** (IA) is used to describe the sum of an organization's IP and IPRs, together with intangible assets such as know-how and reputation.

An organization's **intellectual asset strategy** should articulate the role of intellectual assets in the business and in so doing give clear guidance to assist decision making.

An organization's **intellectual asset policy** should clearly define those actions that are either mandated or prohibited.

An organization's projects, products and services should have fit-for-purpose **intellectual asset plans** identifying the actions that must be undertaken to manage the intellectual assets they will either generate or access. While addressing the interests of the project, product or service it supports, an intellectual asset plan must also comply with the organization's intellectual asset strategy and policy as described above.

THE GOALS OF INTELLECTUAL ASSET MANAGEMENT

PricewaterhouseCoopers have described **intellectual asset management** (IAM) as an ongoing, structured management process that enables businesses to take full advantage of their patents, trademarks, copyrights, trade secrets and proprietary know-how to create opportunities that will ultimately increase shareholder value and improve competitive position.[1] As such, integrated intellectual asset management (IAM) should seek to:

- minimize third party access to, and freedom to exploit, key intellectual assets;
- ensure ongoing access to, and freedom to exploit, key intellectual assets;
- raise the visibility of, and ensure full exploitation of, key intellectual assets.

Each of these objectives can be broken down into a number of tasks as described below.

Minimizing third party access to, and freedom to exploit, key intellectual assets

This involves:

- developing internal systems to maintain the confidentiality of trade secrets and proprietary information;
- winning intellectual property rights, such as those afforded by patents and trademarks;
- monitoring commercial activities of third parties to ensure they are respecting your intellectual property rights.

Ensuring ongoing access to, and freedom to exploit, key intellectual assets

This involves:

- ensuring externally and internally sourced intellectual assets will continue to be available as required;

---

1   D.A. Spieler, PricewaterhouseCoopers, *Intellectual Asset Management Practice*, Boston.

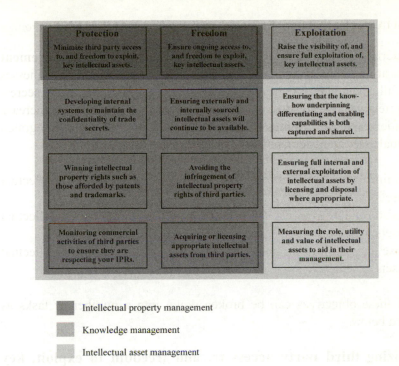

Protection	Freedom	Exploitation
Minimize third party access to, and freedom to exploit, key intellectual assets.	Ensure ongoing access to, and freedom to exploit, key intellectual assets.	Raise the visibility of, and ensure full exploitation of, key intellectual assets.
Developing internal systems to maintain the confidentiality of trade secrets.	Ensuring externally and internally sourced intellectual assets will continue to be available.	Ensuring that the know-how underpinning differentiating and enabling capabilities is both captured and shared.
Winning intellectual property rights such as those afforded by patents and trademarks.	Avoiding the infringement of intellectual property rights of third parties.	Ensuring full internal and external exploitation of intellectual assets by licensing and disposal where appropriate.
Monitoring commercial activities of third parties to ensure they are respecting your IPRs.	Acquiring or licensing appropriate intellectual assets from third parties.	Measuring the role, utility and value of intellectual assets to aid in their management.

▉ Intellectual property management

▉ Knowledge management

▉ Intellectual asset management

Figure 2.1   The integration of intellectual and knowledge management

- avoiding the infringement of third party intellectual property rights;
- acquiring or licensing appropriate intellectual assets from third parties.

Raising the visibility of, and ensure full exploitation of, key intellectual assets

This involves:

- ensuring that the know-how underpinning differentiating and enabling capabilities is both captured and shared;
- ensuring full internal and external exploitation of intellectual assets, making use of licensing and disposals where appropriate;
- measuring the role, utility and value of intellectual assets to aid in their management.

As shown in Figure 2.1, some of these activities are normally carried out under the banner of intellectual property management, while others are addressed by knowledge management. Intellectual asset management therefore requires that both disciplines work as an integrated whole to meet the needs of the organization.

CHAPTER 3

INTELLECTUAL ASSET STRATEGY

Before discussing the content, and function, of an intellectual asset strategy it is useful to develop a clear picture of what is meant by a *strategy*. This understanding can be aided by considering what is meant by a business strategy; one valid definition is: *A business strategy articulates the direction of the business with sufficient clarity to give a clear framework for decision making.*

Thus an intellectual asset strategy can be thought of as a *document that articulates the role of intellectual assets in the business, and in so doing provides a clear framework for decision making.* However, a strategy should not be concerned with the detailed actions that are driven by the needs of, and commissioned by, individual projects; but instead by the actions that are in the interests of the organization as a whole and would otherwise be overlooked by individual projects.

Accepting this definition it is clear that an intellectual asset strategy should provide decision makers with information, guidance and goals. Such a strategy would therefore be expected to address issues such as:

- What are the organization's key capabilities and how the underpinning intellectual assets are to be protected, that is, where "patent estates" should be established to protect core competencies, where secrecy will be used to maintain competitive advantage, and so on.
- Where licensing is to be undertaken for strategic reasons such as: to establish a technology as an industry standard, to share risks and uncertainties inherent in product development and launch, to provide for faster/wider market entry, and so on.

- Where there are gaps in the knowledge base and how these are to be filled.
- Whether patents will be sought to protect inventions that would be invisible in use: that is, an organization may decide it will patent inventions that are visible in manufactured products, but not if they are only used in the manufacturing processes. This course may be taken because of the difficulty an organization will experience in monitoring for infringement in the latter case.
- Where, and how, house marks[1] are to be used and developed.

The core themes covered by an intellectual asset strategy will clearly vary from organization to organization. However, in all cases if a strategy is to add value, it should focus on areas where shortcomings exist or direction is needed. When this is achieved the vision presented in an intellectual asset strategy will provide guidance, where this is needed, to decision makers at the project, product or service level. The function of an intellectual asset strategy is therefore to:

- help decision making (for example, decisions on patent coverage will be aided by a strategy that indicates where given products or services will be marketed);
- place limitations on the decisions that can be made by departments and functions (for example, it will indicate the areas in which information should not be released to a third party, even if this is in the interests of an individual project).

MISUSES OF THE TERM "STRATEGY"

Many different types of document masquerade as strategies. Clearly important projects, products and services should each have an action-plan describing how the intellectual assets they generate or access will be managed. However, if these working-level documents simply describe detailed actions, rather than strategic imperatives, they should be termed plans rather than strategies. Such intellectual asset plans flow out of an organization's intellectual asset strategy and should be demanded, and reviewed, by the organization's decision-making systems. Chapter 12 looks at the contents of intellectual asset plans in more detail.

---

1   House marks is a term used to define the trademarks used by the organization as a whole, rather than the trademarks used for individual products or services.

It should also be stressed that an intellectual asset strategy should not simply be a description of those management processes and competencies needed by an organization to effectively manage its intellectual assets. While an organization should consider the adequacy of these processes, and how they will be strengthened, this is not part of an intellectual asset strategy.

Such intellectual asset management processes are described in Chapters 8 through 11, and include:

- patent committees;
- knowledge databases;
- inventor reward schemes;
- how the costs associated with seeking and managing IPRs will be met;
- the role, organization and reporting structure of the IP/IA function.

As shown in Figure 3.1, intellectual asset strategies therefore have a different focus and function from intellectual asset plans and processes.

THE CONTENTS OF AN INTELLECTUAL ASSET STRATEGY

In order to describe the role of intellectual assets, and hence guide decision making, the strategy will need to identify the key issues facing intellectual asset management within the organization. This may include:

- whether competitors, customers, suppliers and distributors would wish to copy or reverse engineer your products or services;
- whether competitors, customers, suppliers and distributors are likely to respect your IPRs, and if not, whether aggressive action should be taken to enforce your rights;
- where intellectual assets are needed as input to joint ventures or other forms of alliance;
- which are the key territories for marketing and or registering IPRs;
- where competitors, customers, suppliers and distributors are innovating and how your organization should respond;
- the role of house brands and how they are to be developed.

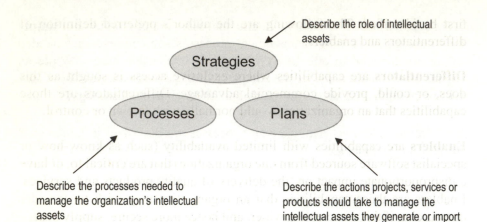

Describe the role of intellectual assets

Strategies

Processes

Plans

Describe the processes needed to manage the organization's intellectual assets

Describe the actions projects, services or products should take to manage the intellectual assets they generate or import

Figure 3.1   The role played by intellectual asset strategies, processes and plans

Using this understanding of the organization's commercial environment the strategy will need to identify key intellectual assets and the actions necessary to ensure their maintenance, enhancement or sharing.

The primary focus of an organization's intellectual asset strategy is often the management of its differentiating and enabling capabilities, where the needs of individual projects, products or services may not be aligned with the interests of the organization as a whole.

As stressed above, if a strategy is to add value, it should focus on areas where shortcomings exist or guidance is needed – especially at the project or service level. In general this guidance is needed in three areas:

- How intellectual assets associated with the organization's enablers and differentiators are to be managed.
- How house marks are to be developed and used.
- The role of licensing in either supporting the existing business plan, or generating income from markets currently not being accessed.

These are explored in the following three sections.

STRATEGIES FOR DIFFERENTIATORS AND ENABLERS

Before guidance can be provided on how to manage the intellectual assets underpinning an organization's enablers and differentiators they must first be identified. The following are the author's preferred definition of differentiators and enablers.

Differentiators are capabilities where exclusive access is sought as this does, or could, provide commercial advantage. Differentiators are those capabilities that an organization would normally wish to own or control.

Enablers are capabilities with limited availability (such as know-how or specialist software sourced from one organization) that are critical to, or have a disproportionate impact on, the delivery of quality products and services. Enablers are those capabilities that an organization may wish to consider outsourcing if this can create a wider, and hence more secure, supply base.

Differentiators and enablers can range from disciplines as diverse as project management, to technical expertise such as an understanding of specific chemical reactions, but will generally underpin a range of products or services as shown in Figure 3.2. Enablers and differentiators are likely to exist in the following areas:

- product manufacture/service delivery;
- the supply chain and its management;
- customer management (attraction/retention/interface).

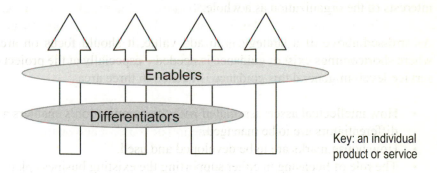

Figure 3.2   Enablers and differentiators will normally underpin a range of products and services

If an organization has a large number of such capabilities it may be necessary to develop a number of stand-alone, capability-level, intellectual asset strategies. Therefore as shown in Figure 3.3, strategies can exist both at the company and capability level; in both cases they will guide decision making at the project and service level.

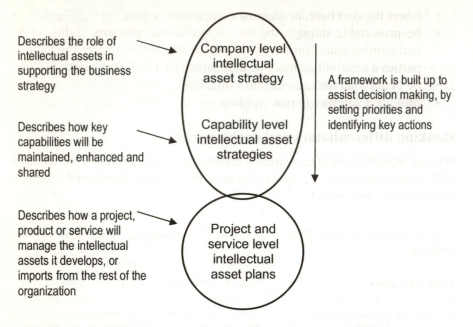

**Figure 3.3   Intellectual asset strategies will feed down to the project, product
and service level**

The identification of differentors and enablers can be aided by the use of
metrics. The characteristics of these capabilities, and hence the metrics used,
will vary from business area to business area, and organization to organization.
The following characteristics are therefore not presented as a definitive list, but
to give an indication of their nature. However, in general, key differentiators
and enablers will often be characterized by capabilities that:

- have application across a range of products/services;
- have a generic and disproportionate impact on cost and quality;
- are important in customer attraction/retention;
- are necessary for safety or regulatory reasons;
- impact on the operation of the organization's product pipeline;
- have high added value/profit generation;
- be critical in the effective management of the supply chain.

In addition, differentiators tend to:

- create a product or service that is genuinely, or perceived by the
  customer base to be, differentiated from other offerings;

- lower the cost base, or increase competitors' costs;
- be protectable through the use of intellectual property rights, or by maintaining confidentiality (without the ability to stop copying by third parties a capability cannot be maintained as a differentiator);
- be better than the competition's offering;
- provide a gateway to new markets.

Ranking differentiators and enablers

Having identified an organization's differentors and enablers it is useful to rank their importance, so that management attention can be correctly focused and resources prioritized.

The following criteria may be of use in developing such a system of ranking.

Differentiators

++	Currently, or likely to become, critical in winning or maintaining market position.
+	Currently, or likely to become, the source of significant competitive advantage.
=	Currently, or likely to become, the source of competitive advantage.
-	Currently, or likely to become, the source of minor competitive advantage.
--	Could become a source of competitive advantage, but role is currently uncertain.

Enablers

++	Maintaining ongoing access is currently, or likely to become, critical in the delivery of cost-effective products and services.
=	Maintaining ongoing access is currently, or likely to become, important in the delivery of cost-effective products and services.
--	Maintaining ongoing access may become important in the delivery of cost-effective products and services.

Having established a list of differentiating and enabling capabilities, and ranked their importance, an intellectual asset strategy will need to address any management actions that would otherwise be overlooked by project-, service- or product-level intellectual asset plans:

*   In the case of a differentiator: actions should be identified to minimize competitors', customers', suppliers' and distributors' access to the capability.
*   For both differentiators and enablers: actions should be identified to ensure ongoing access and freedom to exploit.
*   For both differentiators and enablers: a champion should be identified who is responsible for maintaining the health of the capability, is empowered to make decisions on whether intellectual assets can be shared with third parties, and so on.

A top-level summary of an organization's capability-level intellectual asset strategy can also be produced so that senior management, or the Board, can gain reassurance that a functioning strategy is both in place and driving decision making. Figure 3.4 shows an example of the format such a report could follow.

LICENSING STRATEGY

Another area that may need to be addressed within an organization's intellectual asset strategy is the role licensing plays in supporting the business plan. Intellectual assets, and especially intellectual property, can be licensed for a number of reasons, including:

*   for money;
*   in a cross license, to enable access to third party's intellectual assets, or to gain rights to their improvements without direct investment;
*   in a cross license with a competitor in instances where your commercial activities are infringing their IPRs;[2]
*   to establish your technology as an industry standard;
*   to share risks and uncertainties;
*   to provide for faster/wider market entry.

---

2   This type of cross licensing is common in the consumer electronics industry where companies often infringe each other's patents, but where cross licensing is a more attractive solution than litigation for all parties.

Capability	Diff or Enabler	Importance	Adequacy of capability	Protected by			Technology suitable for license to non-core markets?	Technology suitable for license to core markets?
				Secrecy	Publication*	Patenting		
Ionic chemistry	Diff	+	strong	Chemical kinetics	no	Yes in US, JP, FR and GB	no	no
Project management	Enabler	++	poor	no	yes	no	no	no
Customer database	Diff	++	strong	yes	no	no	no	no
Quality inspection	Enabler	+	adequate	no	yes	no	yes	yes

* An organization may decide to publish information on its inventions because either it wants to avoid others taking out patents, or because it wants to encourage the invention to be developed by others.

Figure 3.4   Top-level summary of an organization's intellectual asset strategy

An organization's intellectual asset strategy will therefore need to define the role of licensing in supporting its business plan, for example:

- The organization may decide that certain market sectors are to be exploited by licensing intellectual assets to third parties, rather than though the direct sale of products and services.
- The organization may decide to license a technology so that it becomes an industry standard, even where this results in a reduced income in some business areas.
- A decision should be taken on whether intellectual property is to be maintained and exploited, through licensing, in areas that are not aligned with existing business activities.

Within this context, an intellectual asset strategy should seek to balance risks (fears) and rewards (greed) from licensing activities. For example:

- How to ensure intellectual property rights are aligned with the needs of licensing.
- How to minimize the loss of control of existing and arising intellectual property.
- How to incentivize licensees, take returns, and cover costs for licences entered into for strategic reasons.

A few organizations have managed to generate significant revenue streams from licensing – such as Dow Chemicals, IBM, Philips, and in the UK, BT – although these continue to be the exception rather than the rule. In general these organizations have been able to generate high license incomes only by deciding to license intellectual property into their core business markets. In other words, a decision has been taken that they are able to strike a better balance between risks and returns by licensing, rather than by seeking to fully exploit every market themselves. The process of identifying both intellectual assets amenable to licensing, and potential licensees, is discussed further in Chapter 14.

The success of these organizations has led to a perception by the management of many others that their intellectual property portfolio can also be used to generate significant license income. However, it should be recognized that not all organizations operate in a market sector, or have access to an intellectual property portfolio, which make possible the generation of worthwhile revenue by licensing. In reality patents rarely produce a license income; surveys have found that only 5 per cent of patents are licensed, while only 1 per cent generates revenue.[3] It should also be noted that, in general, know-how will be the principal asset being licensed. The role of patents is typically to provide a monopoly for the licensee when exploiting licensed know-how. Therefore, patents will typically be of little value unless there is underpinning and valuable know-how, data and information.

Where an organization has decided to pursue licensing, then its intellectual asset strategy should also identify responsibilities and resources necessary to succeed.

PATENT STRATEGY

Any actions connected with patents that underpin enablers and differentiators will be addressed within the strategies prepared for such capabilities. However, there are generally a number of issues that may be best addressed at the company level. For example:

- Should inventions that would not normally be visible in the market place be patented? Some organizations decide that it is only worth filing patents to protect inventions where infringement can be easily spotted. This will often mean patents on manufacturing processes are not filed.
- Which are the default filing programmes for particular business sectors?
- Should inventions that are not aligned with the businesses' current business plans be protected by patenting?

TRADEMARKS STRATEGY

Ideally a brand should help an organization convey a vision of its values, and hence unite all its products and services into a consistent offering. For instance:

- The easyJet brand communicates an image of a low cost, no frills service.

---

3   E. Kahn, 'Patent Mining in a Changing World', *Intellectual Asset Management*, Sept/ Oct 2003.

- The British Airways brand communicates an image of an expensive, but traditional and high quality service.
- The Sony brand communicates an image of innovation and style.

The strongest brands can span multiple market sectors and nations, and can even help connect and motivate employees. However, brands can also convey a negative image, for instance, McDonald's has now become synonymous with an unhealthy lifestyle, and a significant investment is being made to reposition the brand.

In selecting a brand it is clearly important that it conveys the image the organization wishes to project. An established successful brand can enable its owner to:

- charge premium prices;
- sell a higher volume of products;
- realize new income streams by "brand strand stretching" into new products or regions;
- improve the ability to attract and retain quality staff;
- negotiate better trade terms;
- gain lower finance costs.

Traditionally a branding strategy will address:

- brand establishment and awareness building
- media planning/buying
- press relations
- corporate events
- publicity
- news management
- promotions and product launches.

A brand strategy should address the development, use and enforcement of the brand, including the role of any supporting trademarks. In the case of trademarks this will need to address:

- which house marks should be registered, and which not. For those that are registered the territories where protection is needed should be identified.

- the actions necessary to ensure the brand and trademark are being correctly used. This may include guidance notes on how the brand should appear, and so on.
- whether the trademarks are to be licensed, and if this is the case, to which organizations, markets and product groupings.

It should be noted that both an image (called a device), or a word (which can be real or invented), can be registered as a trademark, and in many instances combinations are used. The above activities clearly apply to both devices and word marks.

CHAPTER 4

POLICY AND ACCOUNTABILITIES

POLICY

Whereas strategy provides a framework to assist decision making, policy describes the stance the organization will take in a range of business scenarios. Therefore strategy can be thought of as providing guidance, while policy ultimately provides constraints. This is best illustrated using a few example intellectual asset policy statements:

- The organization will respect valid third party intellectual property rights.
- The organization will vigorously enforce its intellectual property rights.
- The organization will not disclose proprietary information to third parties, unless this is in the interests of the organization as a whole.
- The organization shall retain ownership of intellectual property generated by third parties on its behalf.

There is inevitably considerable variation in the detail presented within different organizations' intellectual asset policies. Some organizations may limit their policy to a series of statements analogous to those given above. However, policy statements of this type are ultimately little more than motherhood statements and as such will rarely aid in the running of the business. Conversely some organizations' policy frameworks may contain very detailed procedures describing not only what should be done but how. When policies contain this level of detail they are often ignored because of the shear volume of information users must navigate to identify their responsibilities.

A policy framework is perhaps at its clearest when it is broken down as follows:

- A number of short policy statements are given defining the organization's stance to a limited number of business-critical scenarios.
- Clear accountabilities are defined stating who is responsible for the implementation and interpretation of this policy.
- Supporting actions are identified in each policy area – ideally describing what should be done, rather than providing a detailed description of the process and methods to be followed. If it is useful to have detailed processes then these are probably best located outside of the policy framework.

Using an example to demonstrate this approach:

Policy	The organization will respect valid third party intellectual property rights.
Accountability	The Commercial Director will ensure that appropriate systems are in place to monitor for third partys' intellectual property rights.
Action	Routine searches will be carried out for published patent applications every two months; these will be commissioned and reviewed by the organization's patent committee. Key words to be used in these searches will be reviewed and updated every two years by the organization's patent committee.

This structured policy and accountability framework clearly defines an organization's approach to important challenges using a clear and simple language.

ACCOUNTABILITIES

The organization's intellectual asset policy should therefore flow down into a clear accountability framework, identifying those responsible for key activities.

The following are a few more examples of the accountabilities that can be placed, probably at Director level, within an accountability framework:

- Monitoring the adequacy of intellectual assets, including licensed rights, to business need and ensure information on strengths, weaknesses, opportunities and threats are appropriately disseminated.
- Maintaining the health, and alignment with business plans, of intellectual assets underpinning the organization's key differentiating capabilities.
- Monitoring competitors' activities to help ensure they do not infringe your intellectual property rights (as it is the perceived, or actual, threat of enforcement that makes intellectual property rights real assets).
- Monitoring and disseminating information on customers', suppliers', distributors' and competitors' intellectual property rights (as this can give a valuable insight into competitors' business strategy).

These accountabilities should normally be placed with that part of an organization gaining the benefit, or pain, of a given decision. However, intellectual assets are not always neatly aligned with a single product or service. Further, where a project's internal ownership varies throughout its life cycle then an inconsistent view may be taken on the priorities – particularly in connection with the expenditure that can be justified when seeking IPRs. Care therefore needs to be taken when defining accountabilities to ensure an appropriate system of checks and balances exists. As a result many decisions in the intellectual asset arena are taken, or endorsed, by committees. Examples include:

- ratifying decisions connected with the protection, maintenance or disposal of intellectual assets;
- developing, and approving, intellectual asset management procedures.

Care should also be taken to ensure that accountabilities are cascaded down to an appropriate organizational level. Using a further example to demonstrate this approach:

Policy	Intellectual assets will be captured, protected, maintained and shared so as to secure maximum commercial benefit to the organization as a whole.
Accountability	Business group directors are accountable for ensuring auditable, fit-for-purpose processes are in place to confirm that intellectual assets are captured, protected, maintained and shared so as to secure maximum commercial benefit to the organization as a whole.

Delegated accountability	Project managers are accountable for commissioning and implementing fit-for-purpose intellectual asset plans.
Individuals sanctioning projects are accountable for challenging the adequacy of a project's intellectual asset plans.
Process owners are accountable for ensuring project approval routes demand the submission, and challenge the completeness, of an intellectual asset plan.

Once this clarity of focus exists, then intellectual asset management (IAM) can be driven forward by challenging and making visible performance of accountability holders.

DIFFICULT PROBLEMS SHOULD BE OWNED

If an organization's intellectual asset policy, and its supporting accountability framework, is well constructed they will help the businesses and functions identify, and prioritize, the tasks they need to carry out to manage their intellectual assets.

A policy framework of this type can be used to ensure that challenging issues are owned, and in each instance a clear position adopted and action taken. For example, the following issues need to be owned and the organization's position periodically reviewed:

- Should there be a system of rewards available to inventors and individuals spotting infringement by third parties?
- Should the cost of seeking intellectual property rights (especially patents and trademarks) be borne by the project, business or held corporately?
- Within a multinational, where should the ownership of intellectual property be placed with view to optimizing the group's tax position?

MONITORING POLICY COMPLIANCE AND THE DISCHARGE OF ACCOUNTABILITIES

To ensure that accountabilities are actively owned, and discharged, it is generally necessary for them to be cascaded down into existing management systems. Specifically, having identified a complete framework of accountabilities an organization should decide which will be:

- included in individual's job descriptions, and ideally appear as measurable performance targets;
- addressed by the inclusion of criteria within management processes, for example, an organization's Stage-Gate system can mandate that project managers submit an intellectual asset plan (see Chapter 5);
- monitored as a compliance issue, with the performance of accountability holders made visible at an appropriate organizational level, which in many cases would be the Board.

The accountability framework can therefore ultimately be represented in the following format.

	Compliance monitored by		
	Job description and performance reviews	Management processes	Part of an annual review reported to the Board
The Marketing Director will monitor the adequacy of intellectual assets, including licensed rights, to business need and ensure information on strengths, weaknesses, opportunities and threats are appropriately disseminated.	Y		
The Head of the patents function will monitor and disseminate information on customers', distributors' and competitors' intellectual property rights.			Y
The R&D Director will maintain the health, and alignment of intellectual assets, underpinning the organization's differentiating capabilities.	Y		
Project managers will commission and implement fit-for-purpose intellectual asset plans.		Y	

CHAPTER 5

DECISION MAKING

Organizations will typically use a variety of formal systems to consider their options and make business decisions. Examples include:

- processes for managing the product pipeline, such as Stage-Gate;[1]
- sales funnel processes, including bid-no-bid tools;
- the S&OP (Sales and Operational Planning) process;
- capital expenditure approval processes such as FEL (front end loading).

These decision-making systems will generally receive, and review, a proposal or business plan. Clearly, such proposals should discuss the health, and management, of their underpinning intellectual assets, ideally by presenting a fit-for-purpose intellectual asset plan.

The contents of intellectual asset plans are dealt with in Chapter 12, but they can range from the complex, to the simple, in which one-line statements are made confirming the absence of issues, for example that:

- no proprietary or confidential information is being released to third parties;
- ownership of intellectual property arising from work placed with third parties will rest with the organization;
- checks have been carried out to help ensure that there is no exposure to liabilities arising from the exploitation of the intellectual assets.

Regardless of their complexity, the accuracy and adequacy of intellectual asset plans should be challenged by an organization's decision-making systems. Unfortunately, within most organizations there is a poor general

---

1   R.G. Cooper, *Winning at New Products: Accelerating the Process from Idea to Launch*, Perseus Publishing, 2001.

understanding of intellectual asset management, and typically not only will any intellectual asset plans submitted be of poor quality, but also the level of challenge applied by decision-making systems will be inadequate. Under these circumstances there will be no pressure to improve the quality of submitted intellectual asset plans. Where this is a problem:

- One or more of the individuals on each approval/review panel can be a trained specialist, with a formal accountability to challenge submitted intellectual asset plans.
- It may be appropriate to develop a number of standard intellectual asset questions that are asked at key stages in the business, product or service life cycle – this is a Stage-Gate type process.
- Model intellectual asset plans, or "crib sheets" giving examples of issues that should be addressed by intellectual asset plans, can be made available to both those preparing and challenging proposals.
- The organization's existing system of accountabilities can be modified to clearly define the responsibility for commissioning, challenging and implementing intellectual asset plans.

A couple of these approaches are discussed below.

STAGE-GATE PROCESSES

Before examining how intellectual asset management can be improved though the use of a Stage-Gate process it is worth exploring the thinking behind this management tool.

Stage-Gate recognizes that projects (*together with products and services*) go through a series of evolutionary stages and argues that, at each of these natural breakpoints, they should be reviewed to:

- decide if the project continues to be worth the ongoing investment;
- monitor the adequacy of the project's execution;
- set or confirm objectives;
- prioritize the project, so that where resources are limited, only key projects proceed.

Each of these reviews, called gate meetings, has a common format.

Inputs: A description of the project and its status.

Criteria: A set of standard questions and criteria used to assess if the project should proceed.

Output: A go/kill/hold decision and an agreed action plan for the project to follow.

There are four types of criteria typically used:

- The project will normally be required to demonstrate that it will make a financial return above a certain minima.
- Projects that have been successful in the past can be studied and their common characteristics identified. New submissions can then be scored against this list of characteristics.
- Measures can be used to capture how acceptable the product or service is likely to be to the customer base.
- The project's fit with the rest of the organization's offerings can be assessed – this approach seeks to ensure that a varied portfolio of projects is maintained.

Each type of criteria has its own advantages and disadvantages. In practice a mixture of criteria or hybrid methods are often used.

As has already been noted the success of most projects will hinge on the health, and management, of their underpinning intellectual assets. It would therefore seem reasonable to expect intellectual asset criteria and questions to dominate gate meetings. However, in practice this is rarely the case. Typically the only intellectual asset question explicitly asked at Gate meetings is "what is the status of patent protection?". This level of challenge is clearly inadequate.

To ensure that intellectual asset management is appropriately addressed by Stage-Gate processes each meeting must include:

- **Input**: Each project should be required to present a fit-for-purpose intellectual asset plan.
- **Criteria**: The criteria and questions used should challenge the health, and management, of the project's intellectual assets.
- **Output**: Any intellectual asset issues that need to be addressed before the project is submitted to the next gate should be defined.

Input

The contents of intellectual asset plans are discussed in Chapter 12, but in essence they should address five issues:

- Is the extent of customer, partner, supplier, distributor and competitor's access to, and ability to copy, key intellectual assets appropriate?
- Are the intellectual assets generated by, or imported into, the project free of third party rights that would hinder their use?
- Will the project's use of intellectual assets have a negative impact on other business activities?
- Will the intellectual assets needed during the project's development be available when required?
- Should the project be importing existing, or sharing arising, intellectual assets with the rest of the business or third parties?

Gate criteria: questions

The questions used at any gate meeting will vary according to the type of proposal considered (R&D project, plant design and build, and so on). For example:

- Project approval routes should, amongst other issues, ask whether patent protection is necessary for commercial success, and if patents are needed whether this protection is in place or being sought.
- Bid-no-bid decision-making systems should, amongst other issues, check if proprietary information is being released to customers and if so, what the impact is on the organization as a whole.
- Approval routes for the use of contractors should, amongst other issues, ask how important the arising know-how is to the organization and whether the work should be carried out internally to ensure such expertise is held in-house.

It is important that these questions are asked at the right point in the proposal's life cycle. For example the impact of releasing information to customers should be addressed before a contract is bid, not shortly before the information is due to be released.

Gate criteria: hurdles

It is often not appropriate to develop hurdle rates for intellectual assets themselves – but instead ensure that the role and impact of intellectual assets are correctly addressed when considering parameters already demanded by the gate meeting. For instance, if an economic value for the project has to be calculated it should take into account:

- the probability of strong patents being granted, and the financial impact of any uncertainty;
- the potential value of the arising know-how to the organization as a whole – not just the project;
- where the release of proprietary information to third parties is inherent in the project's execution, then the financial impact to the organization of such release must be considered.

Gate criteria: tick boxes

It is also possible to use standard questions, of the type discussed above, to prompt projects to highlight and discuss key issues within their submissions to gate meetings.

One such a question could be *"Have databases and communities of practice been used to search for data, information, designs, best-practice, lesson-learnt, and so on?"* Clearly if this cannot be answered affirmatively then the project will have to explain why such action has not been taken.

Questions of this sort can be developed to form a checklist, or even a series of tick boxes. Lists of this type will:

- enable projects to quickly identify the actions they should be taking;
- enable those reviewing proposals to identify areas where they need to challenge the project's performance.

An example set of tick boxes is shown in Figure 5.1.

INTELLECTUAL ASSET TICK BOXES

Basic questions:

- Is the extent of customer, partner, supplier, distributor and competitor's access to, and ability to copy key intellectual assets appropriate?
- Are the intellectual assets generated by, or imported into, the project free of third party rights that would hinder their use?
- Will the project's use of intellectual assets have a negative impact on other business activities?
- Will the intellectual assets needed during the project be available when required?
- Should the project be importing existing, or sharing arising, intellectual assets with the rest of the business or third parties?

KNOWLEDGE MANAGEMENT

Have databases and Communities of Practice been used to search for data, information, designs, best-practice, lesson-learnt and so on? *Has, or will, the identified know-how be imported into the project?*	Yes / For Discussion
Will the project give rise to know-how that should be captured and disseminated internally and externally? *Do specific actions and funds need to be defined for this activity?*	No / For Discussion
Are there skills or information shortages that could impact on the project's delivery? *If so, in which areas, and could these impact on other projects?*	No / For Discussion
Will the project have access to customer, partner, supplier or competitor's know-how that should be imported into the company via this project? *If so, how is this to be managed?*	No / For Discussion
Does the project make use of any of the organization's differentiators or enablers? *If so, which ones were, or will be, accessed and have any shortcomings been identified*	No / For Discussion

PROTECTION

Will the project release commercially sensitive or valuable information to customers, visitors, partners, suppliers, competitors or the public domain, and so on? *If so, have effective actions been taken to minimize migration? Further, do the benefits of continuing with the project outweigh the risks?*	No / For Discussion
Will the commercial success of the project depend on patents, trademarks or registered designs? *If so, are the existing, or anticipated, IPRs of sufficient strength?*	No / For Discussion
Is there a plan describing how innovations will be managed – that is, secrecy, publication or seeking IPRs – and are the costs justified? *Are routine checks made for these innovations – including any the company may have rights to in the supply chain?*	Yes / For Discussion
Are third party's activities monitored to identify any potential infringement? *Have any instances of potential infringements been identified?*	Yes / For Discussion

CONTRACTUAL ISSUES

Will the project, or the organization, be required to give IP warranties, guarantees or indemnities? *If so, what is their value and have appropriate approvals been given? Can any risks be laid-off?*	No / For Discussion
Should the project be asking for IP warranties, guarantees or indemnities from third parties? *If these are being given, can they be relied on?*	No / For Discussion
Is IP being provided by third parties or Group companies? *If so, has agreement been reached on royalties/ transfer pricing, liabilities, onward release of IP and ownership of arising IP?*	No / For Discussion
Will the project give rise to valuable IP that the company will not own, or have appropriate rights to? *Is this position acceptable? If not, what action can be taken?*	No / For Discussion
Does licensing have a role in the project's business plan, or in the generation of revenue/work outside of the project? For example, can licensing be used to increase market penetration (speed/volume), can the customer be charged for access to intellectual property (that is, as an allowable cost), and so on?	No / For Discussion

THREATS

Has the project imported intellectual assets from third parties? *If so, have appropriate rights been secured to enable their exploitation?*	No / For Discussion
Could third party IPRs exist that could stop the project's deployment? *If so, should, or has, a due diligence been performed?*	No / For Discussion
Are key intellectual assets shared with partners? *If so, should, and have, contingency plans been developed against a breakdown of this relationship?*	No / For Discussion

Figure 5.1   Intellectual asset tick-boxes

CHAPTER 6

PEOPLE AND BEHAVIOUR

Intellectual asset management, and especially intellectual property management, is typically regarded by employees and management as someone else's responsibility – an activity that should be carried out by a central function without their input. The reality is different: intellectual asset management (IAM) is the responsibility of almost everyone in an organization. Intellectual asset management requires and produces a trained workforce, aware of their roles and responsibilities. However, in practice establishing this awareness, and developing the necessary skill-base, is often the rate determining factor when seeking to improve an organization's intellectual asset management.

This is important because most of the detailed, supporting, actions described, or implied, by this book should not be carried out by full-time intellectual asset specialists but instead by individuals as part of their normal role. For example:

- Marketing personnel should be aware of the general coverage afforded by their organization's patent portfolio so that they can identify potential infringement when monitoring competitors' activities.
- Project managers, or the resources at their disposal, should have sufficient general knowledge of intellectual asset management to be able to draft and implement an intellectual asset plan.
- Inventors should be able to access externally available patent databases to help monitor the technology development of third parties.

Individuals clearly need to be aware of where they have such responsibilities, have the necessary skills (or access to training) and be subject to performance monitoring. This can be achieved by a mixture of initiatives including:

- Where appropriate, job descriptions should mandate knowledge of intellectual asset management. This will be aided if the organization already uses a system of technical competencies which describe the skills individuals in given jobs should possess and demonstrate (see below).
- Training should be available – especially to help employees generate intellectual asset plans (here training can be supplemented by providing "model" intellectual asset plans).
- Intranet sites can be established providing information to both those with specific intellectual asset accountabilities, and also those who wish to improve their understanding of this topic.

An improved understanding of intellectual asset management will also serve to enhance the visibility of the intellectual property and other legal functions, and hence to facilitate their involvement in decision making.

TECHNICAL COMPETENCIES

Where organizations make use of a competency framework to define the skills specific employee groups should possess, consideration should be given to including intellectual assets skills within this framework. Example skills that can be inserted into existing technical competencies include:

Targeted employee	Intellectual asset skills
Project manager	Is able to identify the key activities projects should undertake to capture, protect, maintain and share intellectual assets to enhance organizational competitiveness.
Inventor	Is able to source information on published third parties' patents, and is aware of recent third party patenting activities in their technical field.[1]
General	Understands, and can describe, his or her role in the protection of the organization's proprietary know-how.

---

1   A few organizations have banned their employees from searching external databases of patents for fear that they will be accused of wilfully infringing a third party's IPRs. This restriction is most common in US companies. However, banning access to such a valuable information source may be an overreaction, especially when employees receive sufficient training to be aware of the dangers.

These intellectual asset criteria can be used within existing competencies; or used to develop new ones specifically targeted at those individuals holding key roles in the management of the organization's intellectual assets. Once in place, career progression can therefore be made dependent on the individual being able to provide evidence that an understanding of intellectual asset management has been developed and applied.

CHAPTER 7

TARGETS AND CHALLENGE

Senior management, or the corporate body, should routinely challenge how effectively intellectual assets are being managed by the operational businesses and the organization as a whole. This, when coupled with the development of clear accountabilities, policy and strategy is an extremely effective method of improving the management of intellectual assets.

Metrics and other indicators can be of considerable use in this process of challenge and, as shown in Figure 7.1, should be used in three areas.

Making visible the alignment of the organization's intellectual assets to business strategy, that is, measuring the role and utility of intellectual assets in key business areas

Making visible the quality of the organization's management of intellectual assets

Setting stretching targets as required to meet the organization's long-term vision

Targets and Challenge

Figure 7.1   Targets and challenge

ALIGNMENT OF INTELLECTUAL ASSETS TO BUSINESS STRATEGY

Although the terminologies used can vary, intellectual assets have two basic characteristics that should be examined:

- **Role**: Here metrics should seek to measure the potential importance of a given asset type to business success (for example, the extent to which trademarks can create a differentiated product that the customer is willing to select in preference to other offerings).
- **Utility**: Here metrics should seek to measure whether a specific asset is fit for purpose (for example, whether the trademark in question has succeeded in creating a differentiated product).

If metrics are used to represent these characteristics, any misalignment between the Role and Utility scores will highlight problems that need to be addressed by management.

The use of metrics will often be restricted to evaluating an organization's key intellectual assets, as it is clearly impractical to generate Role and Utility metrics for all assets. Metrics therefore tend to focus on two areas:

- patents – because of their high cost;
- the intellectual assets that support key differentiators and enablers (see definition on page 13).

Chapter 16 examines the methods that can be used to produce these Role and Utility scores.

THE QUALITY OF INTELLECTUAL ASSET MANAGEMENT

The quality of an organization's intellectual asset management should also be monitored. Here the use of metrics can provide an auditable trail not only identifying deficiencies in the organization's intellectual asset management, but also to highlight best practice.

Some metrics will take the form of simple checks, which will have a "yes" or "no" answer, for example:

- Are accountabilities clear, and if delegated, are approval and reporting structures clearly defined?
- Are responsibilities for the management of intellectual asset captured in appropriate job descriptions and are routine assessments made of whether individuals have the necessary skills?
- Have the organization's key enablers and differentiators been identified and do intellectual asset strategies exist for each?
- Are the hurdle rates imposed by the need to seek funding for intellectual property protection, especially patents, regularly reviewed and judged to be appropriate?

Metrics of this type thus serve to provide guidance on the specific activities each business area should be undertaking.

Metrics can also be developed to show how effectively intellectual asset management systems are being applied. For example, the quality of intellectual asset plans being submitted to project approval routes can be indirectly monitored and presented graphically as shown in Figure 7.2.

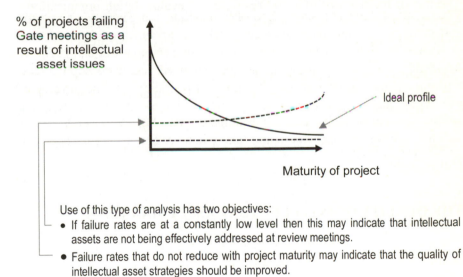

Figure 7.2   Use of metrics to assess the quality of intellectual asset plans

Figure 7.3 identifies seven areas where it may be appropriate to develop a series of detailed metrics. By measuring the performance against these metrics an overall score can be generated in each of these seven areas. In this instance simple red and green symbols are used to represent these overall scores.

Summaries of this type will enable senior management, or the Board if appropriate, to quickly gain an understanding of the organization's overall performance, and the main areas requiring attention.

STRETCHING TARGETS – CONTINUAL IMPROVEMENT

The metrics described above only monitor how well an organization's existing intellectual asset management systems are working.

Step increases in performance generally require changes to be made to systems. This is the domain of the balanced scorecard.[1]

The balanced scorecard is a method of translating an organization's mission and strategy into tangible, measurable, targets. Specifically, this approach seeks to identify targets which, if met, will enable an organization to achieve its strategic objectives. In so doing the balanced scorecard supplements traditional financial measures with a mixture of indicators. The developers of this approach, Kaplan and Norton, write: "The scorecard puts strategy and vision, not control, at the centre. It establishes goals but assumes that people will adopt whatever behaviours and take whatever actions are necessary to arrive at these goals."[2]

---

1   R.S. Kaplan and D.P. Norton, *The Balanced Scorecard: Translating Strategy into Action*, Boston: Harvard Business School Press, 1996.
2   Ibid.

Target	Status	Key actions and timetable
Decision making: Do the company's key decision-making processes and bodies receive information on, and take due account of, the sufficiency of the available intellectual assets and the quality of their management?	◉	Xxxx xxxx xxxxx xxxxxx xxx xx xxxx xxx xxx xxxxx xx xxx xx xxxxxxx. Xxxx xxxx xxxxx xxxxxx xxx xx xxx xxx xxxxx xx xxx xxxxxxx. Xxxx xxxx xxxxx xxxxxxx xxx xx xxx xxx xxxxx xx xxx xxxxxxx.
Policy and accountabilities: Has a clear company policy been set with matching accountabilities to identify key management actions and their ownership?	◉	Xxxx xxxx xxxxx xxxxxx xxx xx xxx xxxxx xxxxx xx xxx xxxxxxx. Xxxx xxxx xxxxx xxxxxxx xxx xx xxx xxx xxxxx xx xxx xxxxxxx. Xxxx xxxx xxxxxxx xxx xx xxx xxx xxxxx xx xxx xxxxxxx.
Strategies: Do strategies exist describing the role of intellectual assets in the organization with sufficient clarity to enable effective decision making; further, is the adequacy of, and changes needed to, management tools described?	◉	Xxxx xxxx xxxxx xxxxxx xxx xx xxx xxx xxxxx xx xxx xxxxxxxx. Xxxx xxxx xxxxx xxxxxx xxx xx xxx xxx xxxxx xx xxx xxxxxxx.
Review and challenge: Are reviews carried out, and appropriately reported, to highlight the health of the company's intellectual asset portfolio and the quality of its management?	◉	Xxxx xxxx xxxxx xxxxxxx xxxxxx xx xxx xxx xxxxx xx xxx xxxxxxx. Xxxx xxxx xxxxx xxxxxxx xx xxx xxxxxx xxxxx xx xxx xxxxxxx.
People and behaviour: Are intellectual asset skills specified for key roles, training provided and competencies monitored?	◉	Xxxx xxxx xxxxx xxxxxx xxx xx xxx xxx xxxxx xx xxx xxxxxxx. Xxxx xxxx xxxxx xxxxxxx xxx xx xxx xxx xxxxx xx xxx xxxxxxx. Xxxx xxxx xxxxxxx xxx xx xxx xxx xxxxx xx xxx xxxxxxx.
Knowledge management: Do knowledge management systems ensure key know-how is identified, captured, disseminated and used?	◉	Xxxx xxxx xxxxx xxxxxx xxx xx xxx xxx xxxxx xx xxx xxxxxxx. Xxxx xxxx xxxxxx xxx xx xxx xxx xxxxx xx xxx xxxxxxx.
IP function: Are the IP function's skills and systems aligned with the needs of the businesses?	◉	Xxxx xxxx xxxxx xxxxxx xxx xx xxx xxx xxxxx xx xxx xxxxxxx. Xxxx xxxx xxxxx xxxxxxx xxx xx xxx xxx xxxxx xx xxx xxxxxxx. Xxxx xxxx xxxxx.

Figure 7.3   Example intellectual asset indicators

The process of building a balanced scorecard normally involves the following stages:

- identifying critical cuccess factors (CSFs) for the organization as a whole;
- developing key performance indicators (KPIs);
- setting targets;
- applying scorecards and targets at the working level.

For instance, one of an organization's strategic objectives may be to increase its market penetration to, say, 20 per cent in five years' time. This objective is broken down into a series of KPIs that, if met, will help achieve this goal. These could include:

- securing distribution arrangements with organization X and Y;
- lowering unit selling price by 5 per cent while maintaining margins.

These KPIs eventually cascade down to initiatives and targets that management can address at the working level, these could include:

- Reducing department costs by 10 per cent.
- Reducing stock levels by 15 per cent.

Clearly, balanced scorecard indicators should be set that involve intellectual assets and their management. However, developing such measures is often challenging. Ideally, metrics describing the quality of intellectual assets should be used within a balanced scorecard. For instance a target could be set in which the average gap, across all projects, between intellectual asset Role and Utility scores (see Chapter 16) is less than 10 per cent. However, because of the subjective way such scores have to be produced, the existence of a target will inevitably influence the scores that are awarded.

As a result, when intellectual assets are considered, targets will often concentrate on:

- measuring the uptake and effectiveness of systems used to manage intellectual assets (as discussed above);

- ensuring that when an organization's performance against generic targets and KPIs is being assessed, due account is taken of the effect of intellectual assets.

In the second case it is important to correctly account for the role of intellectual assets in the achievement of the organization's CSFs, KPIs and targets. In practice it is very easy to lose this focus, as becomes apparent when considering the four areas where targets are traditionally identified, specifically:

- *Financial*: Here targets could include a specified profit margin or turnover for specific businesses, products or services.
- *Customer*: Here indicators are set for such factors as the rate of customer retention and market share.
- *Internal Business Processes*: This area will be characterised by indicators focusing on the performance of a range of business processes. These could include processes used to identify market opportunities, deliver products or manage post-sale actions. Targets could therefore include speed of stock turnover, number of new products in the product pipeline, or the number of returned goods.
- *Learning and Development*: Here indicators will focus on the skills and systems required to deliver the previous scorecard targets. Targets could therefore include measures of employee skills or the completeness of business-critical information.

Intellectual assets clearly have a role in each of these areas. Care should be taken that this inter-relationship is highlighted and recognized in producing targets and metrics. For example, where profit forecasts are made these should include the cost of seeking intellectual property protection (even if this is met corporately), and take into account the risk, and financial consequence, that the IPRs eventually won will be weaker (or stronger) than anticipated.

Targets should also be set in the Internal Business Process and Learning and Development areas. For example:

- 90 per cent of professional staff to have completed an IP awareness course by year xxxx.
- 90 per cent of projects to have a post project review identifying intellectual assets that should be captured on knowledge management systems by year zzzz.

- Intellectual asset Utility and Role scores to be determined for all differentiators by year xxxx.
- 20 per cent of the organization's differentiating capabilities to be covered by the organization's intellectual asset plan by year yyyy.

THE ROLE OF THE CENTRE?

Clearly a function, or individual, needs to be responsible for setting targets and monitoring performance.

With the increasing trend for organizations to create autonomous business units, the corporate body's role is often limited to strategy development and the process of review and challenge. In such an environment the role of the centre should therefore include challenging how effectively intellectual assets are being managed by the operational businesses, and the health of the intellectual asset portfolio, using metrics similar to those discussed above.

This is explored further in Chapter 16.

CHAPTER 8

PROCESSES – KNOWLEDGE MANAGEMENT

Knowledge management has passed through a number of evolutionary stages since its first appearance. Initially the focus was on IT systems created to store, index, and make available an organization's existing documentation. However, knowledge management is now a great deal more than simple document management. Creating massive databases of raw information, while of some utility, will rarely be sufficient to ensure an organization actively shares its knowledge assets. There are perhaps four further elements to modern knowledge management:

- The identification of key know-how, and the creation of summaries designed to increase its visibility. This activity should rarely seek to capture detail, but simply describe the capability, its applications, and contact points. These capability summaries can be stored and shared on a central database.
- The formation of communities, in targeted areas, that are encouraged to share both problems and solutions across normal organizational structures.
- Tacit knowledge can be codified and captured if this is necessary to facilitate its sharing or preservation. However, it is important to recognize that most tacit knowledge cannot be effectively captured, and therefore this option should be pursued with care.
- Maintaining an overview, often captured as a knowledge map, not only of an organization's knowledge base, but also its strengths and weaknesses.

This last activity also enables an organization to target its resources, in what can be thought of as a focused approach to knowledge management as shown in Figure 8.1.

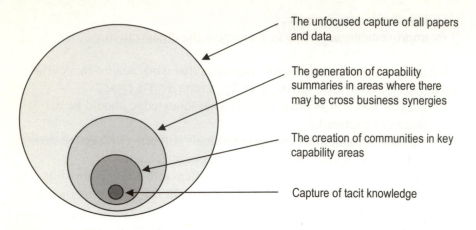

The unfocused capture of all papers and data

The generation of capability summaries in areas where there may be cross business synergies

The creation of communities in key capability areas

Capture of tacit knowledge

Figure 8.1   Providing knowledge management with a focus

The creation, capture, sharing and renewal of knowledge are clearly critical to the delivery of innovative, and cost-effective, products and services. Despite this dependency, as is the case with intellectual asset management, the processes and practices used by organizations to manage their knowledge assets are often disconnected from those employed to manage the services and products they underpin. This disconnect creates a perception that knowledge management is an optional, add-on, activity rather than a core part of an organization's operation.

Further, most organizations wrongly focus purely on capturing, and making visible, knowledge. Knowledge management should be equally concerned with ensuring processes and practices incentivize individuals to share knowledge. This shift in focus is required to address what many see as the biggest challenge facing knowledge management: individuals, and hence businesses and functions, invariably show a reluctance to look for knowledge outside of their local, well-established, networks.

THE CAPTURE AND SHARING OF INFORMATION

Knowledge management must facilitate access to information, skills and competencies. There is clearly a virtuous cycle that organizations will wish to create, whereby:

- key knowledge is made visible across the organization;
- captured and tacit knowledge is applied;

- improvements are made;
- improvements are made visible across the organization.

It is equally clear that there will be pressures that work against this cycle:

- *Lack of focus*: it is often unclear what knowledge should be actively shared or captured.
- *Lack of time and low priority*: individuals will often not see the sharing and capture of knowledge as a business-critical activity.
- *Not invented here*: individuals are often reluctant or unwilling to look for help and use systems that highlight the lessons learned from previous work.

The Fifth Discipline as described by Peter Senge[1] advocates the use of "system diagrams", as shown in Figure 8.2, to represent virtuous and slowing pressures of this type.

Only through an understanding of this knowledge management "system" and specifically the processes that either encourage, or hinder, the sharing of knowledge, will a given organization be able to identify those actions and processes needed to encourage individuals to share knowledge.

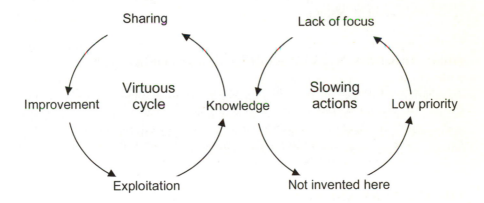

Figure 8.2   **The knowledge management systems diagram**

Examples of activities that can be introduced to overcome these "slowing actions" include:

1   P. M. Senge, *The Fifth Discipline: The Art and Practice of the Learning Organization*, Random House Business Books, 1993.

- *Not invented here*: Project, and other, approval routes can be used to formally check whether projects, products and services have used knowledge databases and Communities of Practice to search for, and import, lessons from previous work.
- *Low priorities*: Accountabilities should be placed to ensure that the actions required to manage an organization's knowledge assets are defined and unambiguously owned. Further, the organization should monitor and make visible how effectively know-how is being managed; this can be aided through the use of metrics and other key performance indicators (for instance, showing the percentage of projects importing from, or exporting information into, knowledge management systems).
- *Lack of focus*: Existing review and approval systems can be used to mandate that projects, products and services review the know-how they have created with view to identify knowledge with potential cross-business application. The progress in capturing, disseminating or advertising this information can then be monitored through the same review systems. However, it is important that an organization maintains a clear vision of the areas where there is benefit in investing in the capture and dissemination of know-how. Therefore, a central function, or a number of expert communities, can be charged with assessing the merits of capturing specific know-how in the organization's knowledge management system.

CLASSIFICATION, TAXONOMIES AND ONTOLOGIES

The classification, indexing and arranging of information so that it can be stored, searched and accessed is a complex subject in its own right. Taxonomies (used to classify information) and ontologies (which are used to describe the relationship between information) are often used as indexes to enable organizations to label and retrieve information.

Ontologies and taxonomies can be thought of as a way of classifying and hence structuring information in a tree-like structure. However, in using such an analogy it should be clear that any item of information can appear in several places in this indexing structure.

Developing an ontology and taxonomy is generally carried out manually, with the categories chosen to describe the nature of an organization's businesses rather than the content of the documents. Ontology and taxonomy therefore tend to be industry specific.

Once created, then either the author, or a central function, can appropriately tag information to assist in its subsequent identification and retrieval. However, the experience of many organizations is that authors often inadequately or inappropriately tag their own work. Therefore, this task may need to be undertaken by a central body or function.

COMMUNITIES OF PRACTICE

Knowledge management should also seek to create processes and structures that foster learning and development. One technique is to encourage the formation of communities that share common problems and solutions across departmental and even company boundaries. By fostering the development of such Communities of Practice[2] an organization can ensure that best practice evolves through the sharing of problems and solutions.

For any organization wishing to create these communities, the initial challenge is often to identify the areas where they should be established. In practice if any of the organization's differentiating and enabling capabilities are organizationally fragmented, then they are the logical focus for the first communities. Such capabilities can cover areas as diverse as customer service advisors and mechanical equipment operators. It should be noted that Communities of Practice formed around differentiating capabilities are likely to involve only the organization's direct employees. Conversely, in the case of enabling capabilities, there may be merit in extending the Communities of Practice to individuals outside of the organization.

Once a community has been identified then the development and sharing of know-how must be encouraged. The approach taken will depend on the nature of the community, but the appointment of a co-ordinator and the arrangement of quarterly meetings and monthly teleconferences may be all that is required to establish a community. At these meetings and teleconferences individuals should be encouraged to share challenges and promising solutions.

---

2   E. Wenger, R. McDermott and W.M. Snyder, *Cultivating Communities of Practice*, Harvard Business School Press, 2002.

In addition to a small highly active core of members, a number of networks are likely to develop within the community that will help maintain the momentum of interaction. Each network is likely to develop its own mechanisms for sharing information, although these are all likely to depend heavily on IT systems.

The role of co-ordinator is essential in the formation and maintenance of these communities. A co-ordinator will:

- develop agendas for meetings and teleconferences by identifying topics for discussion;
- organize venues for meetings;
- help to identify and link communities.

When setting up a Community of Practice the correct choice of co-ordinator is therefore vital. They must have networking skills, a technical understanding of the issues facing the community, and most importantly, the time and interest needed to drive the community forward. However, simply setting up a network and expecting them to suddenly share knowledge is naïve, although this is a mistake many knowledge management professionals fall into. In practice, individuals rarely will be persuaded to adopt knowledge management practices by reasoned argument, but instead need to be forced to change. It is therefore important that these Communities of Practice are given a formal role. For example, they can be used to peer review: research proposals, bid documents, specifications, and so on. By giving these communities specific tasks to perform, they are forced to co-operate and work together.

KNOW-HOW GAPS

Knowledge management should also include a SWOT (strengths, weaknesses, opportunities and threats) analysis of the organization's knowledge base.

As an objective this can initially seem overwhelming. However, this analysis can initially be carried out at a low level; either within the above Communities of Practice, or at the level of the organization's enablers and differentiators. In either case the analysis can focus on:

- identifying the key knowledge, skills and competencies needed to execute the business plan;

- comparing the organization's knowledge to that of its competitors, customers, distributors and suppliers and considering any implications this has at the company, project or service level;
- developing a strategy for closing any gaps.

THE KNOWLEDGE AUDIT AND STRATEGY

A knowledge audit is designed to identify, locate and map the main sources of explicit and tacit knowledge in an organization. Such an activity should also chart the main flows of knowledge, and any deficiencies in these processes. Dr Ann Hylton rightly describes a knowledge audit as an audit of knowledge and not an audit of information, documents or KM systems.[3] The main deliverable from such an audit is, perhaps, the identification of areas where value can be generated through the active management of knowledge assets.

A knowledge audit is normally conducted using a series of face-to-face interviews:

- As a first stage it is necessary for the auditors to gain an insight into the generic importance of knowledge in the delivery of products and services, and also how effectively knowledge is currently being leveraged. Such an understanding is normally developed through a series of short interviews with a cross section of individuals at all organizational levels.
- More detailed interviews can then be conducted to identify, locate and map the organization's main sources of explicit and tacit knowledge. It is clearly important to identify those knowledge assets that are critical in the delivery of products and services.

Such an exercise is a major undertaking. Further, those carrying out the audit will need to understand the business with sufficient clarity to challenge, interpret and cross-check the opinions expressed by the interviewees. Auditors will therefore need to be not only good facilitators, but also have a strong business and technical background. This is not an easy skill-set to source, and this is the reason why many knowledge audits fail to deliver what they promise.

---

3   The knowledge audit is first and foremost an audit, Dr A. Hylton, July 2004, www.annhyton.com.

Ultimately, such an audit should highlight knowledge that is either underemployed or deficient in some way. This insight can be used to provide the focus for a knowledge strategy, by identifying where there is a cross-business need to:

- create Communities of Practice;
- fill knowledge gaps;
- tighten up systems used to manage the release of information to prevent the loss of proprietary information;
- capture tacit information.

As discussed in Chapter 3, a strategy should not be concerned with the detailed actions that are driven by the needs of, and commissioned by, individual projects; but by the actions that are in the interests of the organization as a whole and that would otherwise be overlooked by individual projects or services. A knowledge strategy will therefore help those responsible for managing projects and services to take decisions on the local development, capture, maintenance, protection and sharing of knowledge that are in the interests of the organization as a whole.

Once a knowledge audit has been completed it should be continually updated; this can be achieved if decision-making systems require projects, products and services to identify the knowledge assets they have, or will access – together with any deficiencies and problems experienced. This information can be used to track and continually update the relationship between projects, products, services and knowledge assets, as shown in Figure 8.3. An organization's list of differentiators and enablers can also be updated by checking how many projects, products and services each underpin.

This process will also help identify areas where Communities of Practice or databases would be of utility in encouraging the sharing of critical knowledge assets.

A SUMMARY OF KNOWLEDGE MANAGEMENT

As shown in Figure 8.4, and discussed above, knowledge management must avoid focusing purely on the development of software and IT infrastructure designed to share information. The focus should instead be on the following activities:

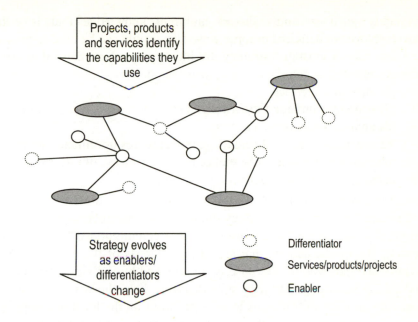

Figure 8.3   A continually evolving knowledge map

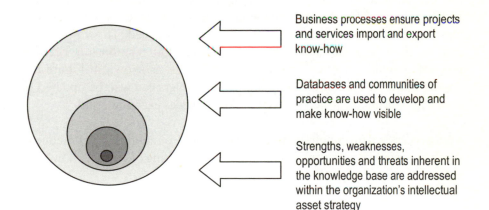

Figure 8.4   Integrating knowledge management into the organization's existing systems

- The use of existing decision-making systems to help identify key knowledge, skills and competencies.
- The use of existing decision-making systems to ensure information is captured, searched for and, where appropriate, used by projects, products and services.
- Developing Communities of Practice in key capability areas to ensure uncaptured know-how is shared.
- The identification of strengths, weakness, opportunities and threats inherent in the existing knowledge base, and the use of this information in the organization's intellectual asset strategy.
- The capture and making available of existing documents.

CHAPTER 9

PROCESSES – INFORMATION MANAGEMENT

At its heart, knowledge management is built on the premise that information must be shared to enable its full exploitation. However, there will inevitably be certain information that is commercially sensitive, and hence its internal and external dissemination will need to be tightly controlled. Organizations must therefore develop processes to ensure sensitive information is identified and its propagation controlled. These processes will need to provide:

- guidance, to enable the sensitivity of information to be quantified;
- an agreed system of labelling;
- clear approval routes for the release of a given item of information;
- clear instructions describing how sensitive information is to be handled.

CLASSIFICATION

Organizations will generally identify several levels, or classes, of commercial sensitivity. Employees will then be given guidance, not only on how to classify any item of information, but also who is empowered to decide on the classification.

For example, an organization may use three levels of commercial sensitivity.

Class (1)

Information that if released to third parties or certain employees, could damage the interests of the organization. Information falling into this classification can be defined, in part, by the use of a non-exhaustive list, which could include:

- business and financial plans
- cost information
- business plans
- proposals
- information on personnel.

Class (2)

Information that provides competitive advantage. Here the listing could include:

- computer source codes
- process data and methods
- calculation methods
- inventions that have not been patented, but where a patent may be sought in the future
- information containing non-public domain, third party information
- organizational charts.

Class (3)

Non-sensitive information. This could be defined as everything that does not fall into Class 1 or 2.

Some organizations may be working with security-sensitive material. Here there will inevitably be a greater number of classification levels such as Top Secret, Secret, and so on. In this case the Government issues guidelines on how to classify and manage information.

It should also be clear who can decide on any information's classification. Again the approach will vary from organization to organization, but one model could be:

- The author can, without consultation, label information as Class 3.
- If the author believes the information should be Class 2, or is uncertain what is the correct classification, then this would be agreed with line management.
- If the author and line manager believe the information should be Class 1, or are uncertain which is the correct classification, then this would be agreed with a nominated accountability holder.

APPROVING THE RELEASE OF INFORMATION

For each class of information, procedures will be needed to define who is able to sanction release to third parties, related entities and employees. In the case of non-sensitive, Class 3, information the organization may take the view that there is no need for a formal system to approve release. However, here there is a risk that information wrongly classified can be released without any formal checks being made.

Where an approval system is felt necessary, then one of the following approaches is generally taken:

- Where there is a fixed list of approvers, chosen to represent a number of key functions, all of whom need to agree on the merit of releasing information.
- Where there is a single point of contact charged with identifying those needing to be consulted before release is sanctioned.
- Where there is a single point of contact who decides, on their own, whether the release is appropriate.
- Where the author and his or her line manager decide on whether the material should be released.

The last of these approaches would rarely be acceptable for the Class 1 material described above, but could be appropriate for Class 3 or even 2. Whether there is a fixed list of approvers, or a "pick-list" used by a central point of contact, the list of approvers is likely to include nominees from the following functions:

- commercial function
- IP and/or legal functions
- technical functions
- the "Owner" of the information
- public relations function
- whoever looks after export controls and/or transfer pricing issues.

An organization will also need to decide whether it should formally approve the release of information when it is covered by a legal agreement such as a confidentiality agreement or a contract. A view may be taken that, for example, the release of Class 1 material to a third party still needs approval even when it takes place against a formal agreement containing obligations of confidentiality.

Where the release of information is an essential part of work being undertaken for a third party then the consequences of its release should clearly have been considered before contractual obligations are entered into. Therefore, the implications of releasing information to customers should be considered at the bid-tracking phase by the organization's bid-no-bid process (not at the point the information has to be released under a legally binding contract). Such a process could, for example, mandate that any Class 1 information likely to be released by a project be identified and its release approved before a bid is made.

Some contracts, especially Government ones, can specify that under certain circumstances the customer has the right to access any information used by the contractor during the performance of the contract. If this is the case, then it may be necessary to consider the implications before sensitive information is used on such projects. Again if this is an issue it should be highlighted in decision-making processes such as bid-no-bid tools and Stage-Gate processes.

HANDLING OF INFORMATION

The handling of sensitive information is a complex subject in its own right. Procedures may be needed to address the following:

- the storage of sensitive information;
- the transfer of paper, and electronic, copies of sensitive information;
- the ownership of sensitive information;
- the clearance of employees before they handle sensitive information.

Storage

An organization may decide that certain classes of information should only be stored on secure IT systems, or in the case of hard copies, locked in certain types of cabinet. There may also be codes of practice stating that such information should not be left unattended on desks, or in the case of very sensitive material, only accessed in secure areas.

There may also be merit in setting a time limit on how long information should be retained, or alternatively defining how frequently its destruction should be considered.

Transfer

An organization may decide that hard copies of sensitive information should be transferred in an envelope that has a return address and a label indicating that it should only be opened by the addressee. However, there is a danger that such a warning could serve to indicate the presence of sensitive material to the curious. As a result, procedures may require the use of an inner and outer envelope – the inner one carrying the notice that it should only be opened by the addressee.

An organization may also take the view that certain information should only be transmitted over the internet if it is encrypted. It may also be necessary to control the onward electronic transfer of such information; in this event there are IT systems that can prevent the forwarding or printing of information if it has been given an electronic "tag". However, such IT systems can be complex and expensive, and are often only worth implementing if a significant volume of highly sensitive material is being handled by electronic means.

Ownership

With highly sensitive information it may be appropriate to track its physical location and record its ownership. In this model each hard copy of a document can be given a unique identification number. This approach is more difficult to apply where information is transmitted electronically; however, it is possible to give a unique electronic ID to sensitive electronic files so that its original owner can be identified if necessary.

Clearance

It may be appropriate to specify which user groups, or individuals, are able to access certain types of information. This can be applied to both hard copy information and information on IT systems. In the case of security-sensitive material, then this approach will clearly be mandated, and certain groups, such as foreign nationals, will be excluded from gaining access.

LABELLING OF INFORMATION

Where information could end up in the public domain, or in the hands of third parties, then it will probably be appropriate to use a copyright legend. There are several forms that can be used; and although their inclusion does not confer extra rights, they do put the recipient on notice that the originator is serious about enforcing its rights. Variations include:

Copyright © Company Name [year article created]

Copyright © Company Name [year article created]

All rights reserved. No part of this publication may be reproduced, stored or transmitted without the written permission of the copyright holder.

Copyright © Company Name [year article created]

All rights reserved. No part of this publication may be reproduced, stored or transmitted without the written permission of the copyright holder.

Warning: The unauthorized use of this copyright work may result in both civil and criminal liability.

Similarly, organizations will generally decide to automatically append a notice to emails reserving their rights. An example is as follows:

This email and any attached files may be commercially sensitive and/or legally privileged. They are intended solely for the person(s) to whom they are addressed. If they have been received by you in error you should not copy, use or show them to anyone. Please reply to this email highlighting the error and then delete the email from your system.

COPYING OF THIRD PARTY INFORMATION

Unauthorized copying of third party information is clearly disallowed by copyright legislation. Such restrictions are obviously warranted where individuals, or organizations, would otherwise undertake large-scale, unauthorized and systematic copying of books, maps, software, and so on.

However, in other instances the restrictions created by copyright legislation can seem excessive. For instance:

- Downloading and printing off information about companies from the Internet, even when it has been placed on the Internet by the copyright owner, will often constitute copyright infringement.
- It is arguable that copying third party patent specifications infringes the patent owner's copyright, even though the patent act clearly envisages such dissemination taking place.

Until recently, many organizations in the UK, relied on "fair dealing" provisions to defend this type of low-level copying; these provisions were included in copyright legislation to allow employees to take a single copy of information for research or private study. However, recent changes in legislation now mean that if the research is carried out for commercial reasons, as is generally the case, they are no longer exempt from copyright legislation.

Similarly, librarians have previously been able to make a single copy of a document for another individual, provided the individual making the request signed a form stating that the document would not be further copied, and it was required for research or private study. This, again, is now only allowed if such research or private study is for non-commercial purposes.

It is therefore very difficult for an organization to be 100 per cent compliant with copyright legislation. Organizations therefore have a difficult line to take when dealing with employees taking one-off copies of short articles and such like:

- They can introduce, and enforce, a policy stating that no copying is allowed without permission of the copyright holder. However, in the extreme, this stance could damage the organization's normal commercial activities.
- They can introduce, but fail to enforce, a policy stating that no copying is allowed without permission from the copyright holder. If infringement is found to have taken place then the employer has the ability to blame the offending employee, and potentially leave them open to disciplinary action. However, this cannot be regarded as good practice.

- They can avoid the subject and hope that employees are sensible in their actions.
- They can take a licence from collecting agencies such as the Copyright Licensing Agency (CLA) or the Newspaper Licensing Agency (NLA).[1]

The position adopted by an organization will often, even if it is not openly admitted, be driven by an assessment of the chances that any infringement will be spotted and action taken. Clearly, if an organization is systematically abusing the rights of other organizations, especially those that make a living from copyrighted products, such as software companies, newspaper publishers or map makers, then not only is the act unjustified, but the chances of falling foul of a law suit are high.

However, an organization may make a judgement that if infringements are infrequent, don't commercially damage the owner of the rights, and are largely against individuals or small companies, then the chances of action being taken are slight. In such cases, there will be little pressure on the organization to introduce a policy that would ultimately limit the activities of employees.

Unfortunately, even where only minor acts of infringement take place, there is still a risk that organizations such as the CLA or NLA may take legal action, in the hope this will encourage others to take a licence.

Although organizations such as the CLA maintain they provide a solution to organizations fearful of infringing others' copyright they, unfortunately, are unable to provide rights to all material, only those that they in turn have licensed rights to. As a result, even organizations with licences from collecting agencies should still insist that their employees check, in each case, that they are free to copy material – this will involve searching a very long list of companies where permission has been given. As a result it is arguable that the procurement of licences from collecting bodies does not really help organizations develop a clear and implementable policy. Instead the cynical may argue that such a licence achieves little other than preventing the collecting organizations from taking legal action.

---

1   The CLA and NLA are collecting agencies. They take licences from various copyright holders and then license these on, as a block, to large organizations. The revenue received is then split between the organizations they take licences from.

CHAPTER 10

PROCESSES – PATENT PORTFOLIO MANAGEMENT

The management of a patent portfolio is often perceived to be unrelated to knowledge, or even intellectual asset, management. However, the experience of an increasing number of organizations shows that the tools and processes needed to manage a patent portfolio can in fact be readily extended to the management of knowledge assets and even all intellectual assets. The effective management of a patent portfolio can therefore be thought of as the first step towards intellectual asset management. This assertion can be explored by examining the tools and processes needed to manage a patent portfolio, thus performing the following tasks:

- spotting inventions and assessing whether, when, and in what territories patents should be filed;
- identifying restrictive third party patents and ensuring they are challenged or circumvented;
- establishing the portfolio's strengths and weaknesses so that opportunities and threats can be addressed within business strategy.

The management of a patent portfolio should therefore not just focus on the patents themselves, but on establishing effective decision-making systems in the organization. Simply taking decisions in a patent committee on what patents to file, renew or abandon is a reactive process only considering inventions bought to the attention of the patents function – as such it cannot succeed in aligning the portfolio to business need.

Patent management must therefore start with an understanding of the processes that can help create a portfolio aligned with business need. Figure 10.1 shows some of the pressures that can either help, or hinder, the creation of this balanced portfolio.

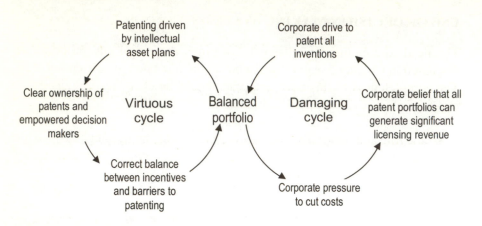

Figure 10.1   System diagram for patent management

As shown, an unbalanced portfolio can result from a range of corporate initiatives that include:

- well-meaning drives and incentives designed to artificially increase the rate of patenting – which can lead to the creation of a large and poorly focused portfolio;
- pressure to reduce expenditure on patents – where cost cutting can lead to valuable inventions not being patented;
- pressure to keep patents in force that are no longer aligned with business need – because of a mistaken belief that they can be sold or licensed, even where the patent portfolio and market strategy do not enable revenue to be generated by this route.

Instead organizations should:

- fine-tune the internal incentives and barriers to filing patenting – such as inventor reward schemes and the ease, or difficulty, with which funding can be obtained for patenting;
- use existing business processes, such as decision-making systems, to highlight inventions that should be considered for patenting;
- ensure clear ownership of patents no longer aligned to core business.

The object of these measures is to ensure that patenting is driven by the quantified needs of products and services, rather than merely responding to received invention records.

USE OF DECISION-MAKING SYSTEMS

The need to submit an intellectual asset plan as part of any proposal, as discussed in Chapter 5, naturally extends to the inclusion of a patenting plan. The completeness of this patenting plan should be challenged by decision-making processes to ensure it addresses:

- the role and importance of patents – are patents being sought to provide collateral in cross licensing, to restrict competitor, customer, supplier or distributor's commercial freedoms, and so on;
- which technology areas should be patented and which should be addressed by secrecy or publication;
- the timing of patent filings and the merit of accelerating or delaying prosecution;
- the territories that need to be blocked to make competitor, customer, supplier or distributor's reverse engineering and copying uneconomic;
- the likely spend on patents and the funding source;
- the timing of, and key words to be used within, searches for third party patents (alternatively the plan should confirm that these are already included within existing patent monitoring processes);
- how potential third party infringement of your intellectual property rights will be monitored;
- whether the planned patenting activity is compatible with the organization's intellectual asset strategy.

As mentioned above, the adequacy of intellectual asset or patenting plans should be challenged by decision-making systems, specifically by asking pertinent questions at the right point in the business, product or service life cycle. For example:

- Project approval routes should, amongst other issues, consider whether commercial success is dependent on patents, and if so whether this protection already exists, or is being sought.
- At the bid tracking stage bid-no-bid decision-making systems should, amongst other issues, consider whether ideas presented in the bid document are adequately protected by patents.
- Approval routes for publishing papers and so on should ensure that any inventions described are either already patented, or their disclosure is consistent with the relevant intellectual asset plan.

The existence of such plans will also enable the patenting function to more effectively prioritize inventions that are brought to its attention. The patenting process is often triggered by the receipt of a signed, witnessed and dated invention disclosure, prepared to formally record the invention and also to enable action to be prioritized. Invention submissions normally contain the following:

- a description of how the invention works, how it improves on prior art[1] and what problems it overcomes;
- any deadlines that necessitate early patent filing;
- a list of inventors and their employer.

When an organization generates a significant number of invention records it can be difficult for the patent department, or individual attorneys, to prioritize their work. However, if the invention submission refers to the patent (or intellectual asset) plan this will enable actions to be quickly identified and prioritized. In addition the clear picture of the business's need for patent protection, that should be presented in these plans, will be of considerable use to the attorneys in the process of patent drafting.

PATENT REVIEWS

Most organizations holding significant patent portfolios carry out periodic reviews into the adequacy of the coverage it affords. These reviews generally involve a mixture of technical, IP and commercial personnel who discuss the merits of individual patents or patent groupings. Formalized process are often developed to produce metrics that assist in decision making; such metrics are described in Chapter 16.

Ideally such reviews should map the patent portfolio on to either the organization's business plan, or its enablers and differentiators. Thus areas where there is currently no, or minimal, patent protection will also be reviewed.

---

1   Prior art is a term used to describe the totality of the information published on a particular area. This represents the area that cannot be patented because it can no longer be regarded as novel.

By following this approach, the role of an organization's patent committee becomes one of challenging and endorsing decisions made by these reviews and other decision-making systems.

Further, the information generated by these reviews can be combined with that in the invention submission, in a standard proforma. If these are collected in a central, indexed, database a powerful tool can be created to make visible the organization's patented technologies, as indicated by Figure 10.2.

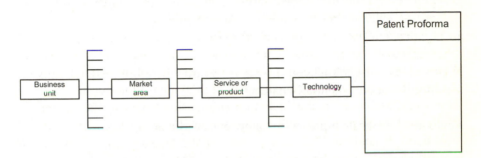

Figure 10.2 Database for indexing and describing patented technologies

Such a database can fulfil a number of additional functions:

- To record the original reasons for filing a patent, together with any relevant decision points – such as proof of concept trials.
- To create a central record showing the utility of individual patents to help make decisions on renewals.
- To identify the benefiting business so that costs can be correctly recovered (where appropriate).
- To record any rights that have been ceded to, or gained from, third parties.
- To aid communication between the businesses and the patenting function.

Further, a patent database of this type can, by including information on non-patented technologies, become the basis of a knowledge management system.

INCENTIVES AND BARRIERS

Organizations will deliberately, or unintentionally, create processes that can either encourage, or hinder, the filing of patents. The two most obvious processes are the ease with which funding for patenting can be secured, and the level of rewards received by inventors.

Rewards

Inventor reward schemes should not be confused with suggestion schemes. Suggestion schemes tend to address improvements to the way in which an organization uses its personnel or existing equipment. Inventor reward schemes should be concerned with discoveries that enable new equipment or processes to be introduced. Inventor rewards therefore tend to focus on inventions that are potentially patentable.

There are three basic types of inventor reward system:

- Schemes that provide inventors with a certificate or other non-monetary token of recognition.
- Schemes that provide inventors with a low level of monetary reward for each patent application filed and/or granted, irrespective of the invention's merit.
- Schemes that provide inventors with a level of financial reward based on the benefit accrued from the invention.

It should be noted that many countries have legislation that force organizations to make a financial payment to inventors. There is considerable regional variation in both the criteria that need to be satisfied before a reward is triggered and the level of any payment. Organizations will therefore need to ensure their inventor reward scheme, as a minimum, satisfies the local legislative framework.

There are several reasons why an organization may choose to introduce an inventor reward scheme to supplement that required by legislation:

- It can provide a visible reward/recognition system to maintain enthusiasm and help create a competitive environment between inventors.
- It ensures ideas are passed through the appropriate channels and any supporting work is progressed with the inventors fully supporting

the patenting process (the process of patent prosecution may require considerable time and effort from the inventor, and some organizations feel this warrants additional payments).
- It can improve employees' awareness of patents and intellectual asset management in general.
- If payments are linked to the commercial exploitation of the patent it may encourage the inventor to assist in the commercialization of their invention.

However, there are also reasons why an organization may decide it is inappropriate to introduce such a scheme:

- Management may take the view that R&D staff are employed to invent, and additional payments should not be required to encourage them to perform their contracted duties.
- Such schemes will tend to preferentially reward employees who are fortunate enough to work on projects where new discoveries would be expected to arise.
- Such schemes may create ill feeling if non-inventing employees involved in a project's commercialization are not financially rewarded for the success of the project.
- The prospect of financial rewards may create pressure to include non-inventors on the list of inventors recorded on the patent application. In the extreme this may invalidate the patent.
- There is likely to be a considerable delay between the invention being made, and its value becoming clear. An organization is therefore faced with a choice between making a premature reward, which may ultimately prove to be at an inappropriate level, or delaying and hence reducing the motivating effect.
- If an organization does not adequately screen inventions prior to patenting, then inventor reward schemes may lead to the filing of patents where there is no, or limited, business need.

Where a license income is being received from a third party then it may be more appropriate for the inventors, and perhaps those involved in the technology's commercialization, to receive a proportion of the income. This royalty splitting arrangement is often adopted by universities, where the net income is typically split between the inventors, the department and the university. In this instance the way in which any royalties are allocated will often vary according to the level of income; when the license fee is low the inventors will generally receive the majority of any income. As the royalty increases, then the proportion allocated to the department and the university will typically be increased.

However, the problems already highlighted with reward schemes remain. For example, there is generally a considerable delay between the act of invention and any income being received; further, care needs to be taken that *all* those involved in commercialization are rewarded, not just the inventors.

In some instances organizations will seek to commercialize their intellectual assets through the formation of spin-off companies. Giving inventors a share of the equity of a spin-off company will not only provide a tangible incentive to encourage their participation in the winning of IPRs, but also ensure their active support in the commercialization process. However, there are disadvantages to this approach that need to be borne in mind:

- It may encourage researchers to occupy management positions within the spin-off company that they are not equipped to perform.
- The inventors may need to be granted a period of leave of absence from their original duties; and ultimately the process of commercialization may result in the loss of key employees.
- Conflicts of interest can arise, and care will be needed both to anticipate and deal with these.

It is clear from the discussion above that the desirability of adopting a scheme for rewarding inventors will vary from industry to industry and organization to organization. A thorough assessment of all the risks and benefits must clearly be made before introducing, or changing an existing, inventor reward scheme.

Funding

The cost of seeking and maintaining patents can be significant and it is therefore important that there is a clear justification for such expenditure. A key factor in ensuring patents are filed only when appropriate is the way in which the costs are distributed within the organization. There are four basic models that can be followed:

- Payment by the corporate body – the costs will be hidden in overheads and not directly recovered from the benefiting business area or project.
- Payment by the benefiting project.
- Payment by the benefiting business area, but without recovery from the specific project.
- Payment by a central licensing function or IP holding company.

The easiest approach to justify intellectually is to require the project to meet patenting costs, as this will ensure that the project's profitability accurately represents all the associated expenditure. However, many organizations find that this can result in a reluctance to seek patent protection, as the associated expenditure can sometimes be difficult to find until the project is relatively mature, by which time it may no longer be possible to win such rights. Conversely, if the costs are met centrally then there may be a tendency for patents to be sought when there is little prospect of a financial return being made.

A further complexity arises if the patent has more than one application within an organization. Where an organization has a large patent portfolio, without a 1:1 alignment between patents and projects, it may be difficult to agree what proportion of expenditure should be met by a given project or even business area.

The following are examples of the factors that may guide the choice of funding route:

- Project funding is probably most appropriate where the returns from patenting are quickly realized, or where there is a strong appreciation of the role played by intellectual assets within the business.
- Business funding is probably most appropriate where there is a reasonable level of intellectual asset awareness, but where the projects will not see a quick return from patenting.
- Corporate funding is probably most appropriate where there is poor intellectual asset awareness in the organization as a whole (and hence the project/business cannot be relied on to make the right decisions).
- Where a central IP holding company has been formed to either provide a focus for licensing to third parties, or to manage the cross licensing of IP within a group of companies (this is discussed in Chapter 13), then it is likely that the costs of patenting will be met by this body.

In practice it is increasingly rare for organizations to fund all patent prosecution corporately. Instead either the businesses fund patenting (in this regard an IP holding function or subsidiary should be regarded as a business), or a system is adopted to split costs between the corporate body and the businesses. One cost splitting option makes use of the delay in expenditure afforded by the Patent Convention Treaty[2] (PCT) route for patent prosecution. The PCT system delays a patent's entry into the expensive national phase for 30 months or more after initial filing. The costs associated with this initial low cost phase can be met corporately, after this point the businesses would be required to meet the costs. This approach has two advantages:

- The delay gives the business the chance to evaluate the technology and the justification for patenting.
- The existence of a patent forces the business to make a decision – specifically, to meet the costs or abandon the patent. That is, it is not possible to inappropriately delay making a decision on patenting.

However, the businesses clearly need to be aware of, and approve, the patent's continued prosecution prior to its automatic publication 18 months after filing – as publication both alerts third parties to the technology and prevents the subsequent withdrawal and refiling of the patent.

OTHER ASPECTS OF PATENT MANAGEMENT

Patent infringement

If an organization commercially exploits, sells, or offers to sell an article or service in violation of a third party's valid intellectual property rights, then it has committed an act of infringement.

There are three types of activity that can be carried out in response to the threat posed by third party patents:

- An intellectual property due diligence (often called a 'freedom for use review') will seek to proactively identify third party rights that could present a legal obstacle to the deployment of a given product or service. With a freedom for use review, this task is carried out at a key point in

---

2   The Patent Convention Treaty gives a patent owner the ability to delay the process of filing a patent in multiple territories.

the product or service's life cycle and updated at appropriate intervals. These reviews can be expensive to perform, but once an organization has reviewed its core technologies, then individual projects need only be concerned with reviewing their new features. The nature of freedom for use reviews is explored further in Chapter 17.

- In the case of patent monitoring regular searches are made for third party patents, published since the last search, using search parameters chosen to match an organization's technical and commercial interests. A check is then made to ensure there are no plans to deploy any of the concepts described in these patents. Over the course of time, patent monitoring can provide a reasonable level of assurance that an organization will not infringe third party patents. However, there is always a danger that an interest in a technology is not established until after a third party's patent was reviewed and subsequently forgotten.

- Do nothing. Some organizations take the decision not to check for third party rights, but instead hope infringement won't be spotted. Also, in some business sectors, organizations collectively choose to rely on their ability to take a licence from any patent owner. This approach works well when there is mutual dependency on cross licensing; where this is the case an infringer can be relatively confident of his ability to get a licence, at a reasonable rate, from most IPR owners.

Routine patent monitoring also serves other purposes:

- It provides information on the technologies being developed by customers, suppliers, distributors and competitors. This not only gives an insight into their likely future offerings, but also gives advanced warning of changes in market dynamics, such as that resulting from an organization broadening or changing its business focus.
- It will give early sight of restrictive third party patents and thus enable, where there are grounds, pre-emptive action to be taken to oppose or challenge their grant.

The choice of approach taken by an organization to deal with these risks is clearly a commercial decision. However, the following should always be in place to ensure the approach taken is appropriate:

- Accountabilities should specify who is responsible for ensuring the adequacy of policy and systems.
- Decision-making systems such as project approval routes and bid-no-bid processes should consider the desirability and timing of a freedom for use review. For example some organizations may decide that as a matter of policy, no product will be launched without it being the subject of a freedom for use review.

Unsolicited inventions

Many large technology-based organizations routinely receive unsolicited inventions from the general public and other sources. These inventions are often sent to senior figures such as the Chief Executive or the Head of R&D.

There are three issues organizations need to be wary of:

- There is the danger that, at some point in the future, the inventor may accuse the recipient of exploiting the disclosed invention without permission. This can become a real danger if the submission parallels work that was already being carried out internally.
- A significant proportion of such submissions will not be aligned with the organization's business, and often describe concepts that violate the laws of nature. Time will often be wasted finding a polite way to respond to the submission.
- Even where the submissions are technically sound it will be difficult to spot those that could be taken through to successful commercial launch without significant investigation. Considerable resources can be wasted in both assessing the utility of the invention and responding to the inventor in an appropriate manner.

If an organization receives a significant volume of unsolicited inventions it may choose to develop a policy for dealing with such submissions. These can range from:

- Responding to all submissions with a polite letter stating that the organization does not accept unsolicited inventions.
- Responding to all submissions stating that the organization will only accept information on an invention if it has been patented. In some

instances the organization may ask for the inventor to waive all rights other than those afforded by patents.

• Filter the submissions, and either state the organization has no interest in the submission, or ask the inventor to sign a confidentiality agreement and, once signed, evaluate the technology in more detail. However, the cost of negotiating a confidentiality agreement and the subsequent evaluation can be significant.

A further issue to consider is whether to keep the correspondence. In general it is probably wise to keep a copy of the submission, so that any subsequent communication from the inventor can be appropriately dealt with.

The stance adopted by any given organization to all of these issues will depend on how many inventions it receives, and the perceived probability that it may eventually receive an invention of value.

Invention disclosure

There may be technology areas where an organization will decide to publish information on its inventions, rather than pursue patents, because:

• while it wants to avoid the risk of third parties taking out patents, it cannot justify the high cost of seeking patents;
• such disclosure may encourage the technology's development by third parties. This position is desirable for technologies that an organization simply wishes to procure from the lowest possible source.

Online specialist journals have appeared to help organizations find a low cost way of achieving this defensive publishing. Research Disclosure and IP.com are two such websites offering on-line publication. These websites are used by several patent offices, and thus examiners should use these sources of information when assessing the patentability of applications they receive from other organizations.

The alternative approach is to file a patent application and then abandon it 18 months after the application date, by which time it will have been published by the relevant patent office. While this arguably results in a disclosure that is more visible to patent examiners, it is a more time consuming and costly option.

As part of its patenting processes and systems, organizations should therefore consider whether it will routinely use on-line publishing or patent abandonment to achieve necessary defensive publication.

CHAPTER 11

PROCESSES – IP AND IA FUNCTIONS

THE IA FUNCTION

Even where there are clear accountabilities, and the majority of employees understand the actions they should take to assist in the management of the organization's intellectual assets, it may still be necessary to identify a number of intellectual asset specialists available to provide technical advice and hold key roles.

These roles can be full or part time, but to prevent these specialists from becoming isolated from the business, and its capabilities, there is often merit in keeping these as part-time roles. There may also be sense in using a matrix management structure in which these individuals have responsibilities both to their employing business and to a central IA function.

Such individuals can hold a variety of roles, including:

- helping others prepare and review intellectual asset plans;
- the identification of cross-business enablers and differentiators, and the generation of matching intellectual asset strategies (this central attention may be warranted because the management of these assets may not be appropriately considered by local processes focusing on individual products or services);
- owning the "health" of key capabilities;
- managing the day-to-day discharge of accountabilities that have been placed at Director level;
- acting as co-ordinators in any Communities of Practice;
- maintaining an overview of the alignment of the intellectual asset portfolio to business need;

- reviewing and challenging the businesses' management of intellectual assets;
- helping patent attorneys gather the information needed for patent prosecution.

An example of how this can work in practice can be found in Dow Chemicals. Dow have established a network of intellectual asset managers responsible for developing and maintaining an intellectual asset plan aligned with business strategy, reviewing the intellectual asset portfolio and identifying know-how that should be captured.[1]

COMBINING THE IP AND IA FUNCTIONS

Clearly, the businesses should take patent filing and maintenance decisions; while the IP function, whether based internally or outsourced, will be responsible for the legal process of drafting, filing and the maintenance of patents.

The role of an internal IP function can be extended to include the IA management activities described in the previous section. There are advantages and disadvantages to combining these roles.

Relationship between the IP function and IA functions

When patents and trademarks are an organization's most important form of intellectual asset then there are sound arguments for the IP function to hold some of the IA management responsibilities described above. However, in this case the IP function will no longer be purely concerned with legal issues, and it may be appropriate to base it in the Commercial or R&D areas, rather than within the legal area.

Where the most important forms of intellectual asset are know-how, data, processes and information, then the IP function will not naturally be involved in their management, and may regard this as a distraction from the pursuit of intellectual property rights. Certainly the technical skills needed to win strong intellectual property rights are different to those required to manage the softer forms of intellectual assets.

---

1   G. McConnachie, 'The Management of Intellectual Assets: Delivering Value to the Business', *The Journal of Knowledge Management*, 1(1); G. Petrash, 'Dow's Journey to a Knowledge Value Management Culture', *European Management Journal*, 14(4).

Splitting the IP function and IA functions

The creation of a separate IA function is particularly appropriate when:

- patents and trademarks are less important than other forms of intellectual asset (know-how, information, processes, and so on);
- the organization does not employ its own attorneys, instead outsourcing this work to private practice.

However, if the IP and IA functions are separate then care needs to be taken that the IP function does not become a reactive service provider, with all management issues and decision making handled by the IA function in isolation. Systems will therefore need to be developed to ensure that:

- attorneys have sufficient contact with the businesses, and the IA function, to understand the role and utility of the patents/agreements/trademarks they are handling;
- priorities and commercial deadlines remain clear;
- attorneys' specialist knowledge is sought and used where appropriate.

Outsourcing patent and trademark prosecution

If the decision is taken to entirely outsource patent and trademark prosecution, and hence not retain in-house attorneys, then there are additional concerns that arise as a result of the lack of in-house specialist legal expertise. In this case there are problems in:

- monitoring the quality of patent drafting and trademark prosecution;
- avoiding unqualified personnel being placed in a position where they are providing quasi-legal advice either directly, or indirectly, by making a judgement on when to seek advice from a patent attorney.

These challenges can be managed if the different functions are appropriately resourced, work closely together, and responsibilities are clearly defined. However, the skill base needed to efficiently outsource patent prosecution will take time to develop.

THE IP FUNCTION

An IP function can range from a single individual, through to a large capability with constituent departments spread across several group companies. Where a large function exists, the following are likely to exist in addition to patent and trademark attorneys.

Formalities

There are number of deadlines imposed by the legal processes of filing patents, trademarks and registered designs. These result not only from the need to make decisions at key points, such as agreeing the territories where coverage is needed, but also the need to supply technical information to the examiners considering the patent or trademark application in the various national patent and trademark offices.

As a missed deadline will often result in a permanent loss of rights, it is vital to keep track of all forthcoming action dates. Tracking these deadlines is a complex task, especially if the patent or trademark is filed in a range of territories.

Fortunately, so-called formalities computer programmes, such as those supplied by IPSS and Pro Delta, have been developed to track key events and deadlines. Where an organization has a large number of cases then a formalities team may be formed to keep the information in these systems up-to-date. Such information is partly generated by the software itself, according to a timetable laid down by national and international legislation, and partly by the formalities team who extract and enter data from the attorney's correspondence. Regular diaries are generated to help trademark and patent attorneys timetable and prioritize their work. Further, by tracking outgoing correspondence, checks can be made by the formalities team that the attorney's actions have been discharged.

By entering additional data, the utility of these diary systems can be extended:

- To record whether the IP is in use, or likely to be used, within the organization.
- To record whether the IP is already licensed to a third party, or whether there are potential licensees.
- To record whether any infringers have been identified.

- To record the attorney's assessment of the actual, or anticipated, strength of the patent.
- By selecting and entering key words to describe each patent, it is possible to identify and track related cases.
- To record the business areas where the IP may be of relevance.
- To identify the project that gave rise to the IP and any key development dates.
- To record the key dates in the prosecution of any third party IP which has been identified as being of concern, thus ensuring any planned opposition is timetabled, and that renewals are monitored to check if the IPRs are being kept in force.

Key information and statistics can then be readily extracted from such programmes and presented to management. Wider distribution of this information may also be warranted, if this could help internally advertise and hence encourage take-up of the technology.

Members of the formalities team can also be charged with:

- providing feedback to inventors on the progress of any patent application;
- ensuring inventors are aware of the information they need to provide to the attorneys and when it will be required;
- monitoring attorney's correspondence to ensure actions have been discharged;
- producing renewal schedules identifying when payments need to be made to keep the IPRs in force.

Renewal agents

The payment of renewal fees can also be managed in-house or subcontracted to external renewal agents such as CPA and Dennemeyer.

Many IP functions have taken the view that tracking renewals and making renewal payments are not core skills and can be safely outsourced. Where external renewal agents are used they will highlight when renewal decisions need to be made, and make payments where instructed to keep the IPRs in force.

Cost tracking

Setting budgets is often one of the biggest challenges facing an IP function. The organization will generally insist that the function's budget is fixed at the start of the year, but unfortunately expenditure can be very difficult to predict. Certain costs can be accurately predicted, such as grant fees and renewal charges. However, labour costs will depend on both the complexity of any given case and the opinions and judgements made by the patent office, and are therefore impossible to predict accurately.

Some organizations use bespoke software, which uses historic information on average costs, to predict expenditure. However, this type of analysis will only provide an accurate forecast when an organization has a large IP portfolio, and hence random factors average out. Where the portfolio is smaller, then problems with a few cases can lead to a significant deviation from forecast costs. However, accuracy can be improved if the predictive tools do not simply rely on average costs, but use information on historic expenditure incurred by "complex, "average" and "simple" cases. More accurate cost forecasts can then be produced if the attorneys tag each case according to how challenging they believe the prosecution is likely to be.

Despite the challenges, this type of analysis is worth using as it not only can be used to set budgets, but also it can help customers decide which case they should support.

Review and challenge

As was discussed in Chapter 7, there is merit in developing metrics, which can be used to set targets, and also monitor the quality of an organization's intellectual property management. This approach should clearly be extended to the IP function. Figure 11.1 uses the same style of presentation as discussed in Chapter 7 to identify a number of areas where KPIs should be used to set goals and monitor performance.

Target	Status	Key actions and timetable
Skill base: Have critical skills been identified, and in each instance robust sources of expertise secured? Are systems in place to prioritize work where there are conflicting pressures on resources?	⊙	Xxxx xxxx xxxxx xxxxxxx xxx xx xxxx xxx xxxx xx xxx xx xxxxxx. Xxxx xxxx xxxxx xxxxxxx xxx xx xxx xxx xxxxx xx xxx xxxxxxx. Xxxx xxxx xxxxx xxxxxx xxx xx xxx xxx xxxxx xx xxx xxxxxxx.
Integration: Is the IP function appropriately networked into, and visible to, the business and R&D functions?	◉	Xxxx xxxx xxxxx xxxxxxx xxx xx xxx xxxxx xxxxx xx xxx xxxxxx. Xxxx xxxx xxxxx xxxxxxx xxx xx xxx xxxxx xx xxx xxxxxxx. Xxxx xxxx xxxxx xxxxxxx xxx xx xxx xxx xxxxx xx xxx xxxxxxx.
Due diligence: Are processes in place to determine the need for, and depth of, due diligence reviews? Further, is sufficient expertise available to assess the impact and threat posed by potentially conflicting third party rights?	○	Xxxx xxxx xxxxx xxxxxxx xxx xx xxx xxx xxxxx xx xxx xxxxxxx. Xxxx xxxx xxxxx xxxxxxx xxx xx xxx xxx xxxxx xx xxx xxxxxx.
Monitoring: Is the prosecution of third party rights monitored and information appropriately disseminated? Do attorneys continuously monitor third party IPRs so that they can be taken into account during drafting?	◉	Xxxx xxxx xxxxx xxxxxx xxxxxx xx xxx xxx xxxxx xx xxx xxxxxx. Xxxx xxxx xxxxx xxxxxx xxx xx xxx xxxxxx xxxxx xx xxx xxxxxx.
Financial control: Are accurate budget forecasts prepared and adhered to? Does the accessibility of funding create the right balance between encouraging and hindering the filing of intellectual property rights?	○	Xxxx xxxx xxxxx xxxxxx xxx xx xxx xxx xxxxx xx xxx xxxxxx. Xxxx xxxx xxxx xxxxxx xxx xx xxx xxx xxxx xx xxx xxxxxx. Xxxx xxxx xxxxx xxxxxx xxx xx xxx xxxx xx xxx xxxxxx.
Data management: Are key prosecutional deadlines and responses tracked and are all appropriate personnel informed of progress? Are timely reminders of key events given to inventors, decision makers and attorneys?	⊙	Xxxx xxxx xxxxx xxxxxx xxx xx xxx xxx xxxx xx xxx xxxxxx. Xxxx xxxx xxxxxx xxx xx xxx xxxx xxxxx xx xxx xxxxxx.

Figure 11.1 Example intellectual asset management indicators for an IP function

CHAPTER 12

PROCESSES – INTELLECTUAL ASSET PLANS

GENERIC IA PLANS

An intellectual asset plan should describe how a given project, product or service will manage the intellectual assets it generates or accesses. As such intellectual asset plans can range from the complex to the simple; but in essence they should all address the following:

- Is the extent of customer, partner, supplier, distributor and competitor's access to, and ability to copy, key intellectual assets appropriate?
- Are the intellectual assets generated by, or imported into, the project (*product or service*) free of third party rights that would hinder their use?
- Will the project's use of intellectual assets have a negative impact on other business activities?
- Will the intellectual assets needed during the project's development be available when required?
- Should the project be importing existing, or sharing arising, intellectual assets with the rest of the business or third parties?

In addressing these issues any actions taken at the project level should clearly be consistent with both the organization's intellectual asset strategy, and its policy and accountability framework.

It is not possible to develop a definitive "model" intellectual asset plan applicable to all organizations and markets. However, the flow chart shown in Figure 12.1 describes a process that can be followed in the production of an intellectual asset plan. The issues that need to be addressed in managing patents, trademarks and software can be more complex, and are addressed in more detail later in this chapter.

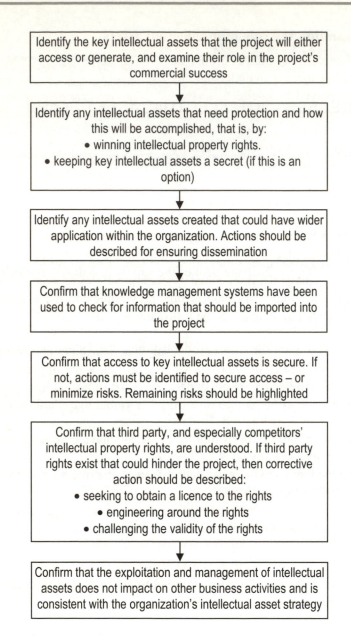

Figure 12.1   The main elements of a project-level intellectual asset plan

Understanding the role of intellectual assets

An intellectual asset plan can only be prepared once there is an understanding of the role played by intellectual assets in its commercial success.

Identify the key intellectual assets that the project will either access or generate, and examine their role in the project's commercial success

Specifically, it is necessary to identify the key intellectual assets that will be used to:

- track opportunities and win work;
- produce and deliver the product;
- create a product that is, or is perceived to be, different from others in the market place;
- ensure effective management of the supply and distribution chain.

Protection

The intellectual asset plan should identify any intellectual assets that need to be protected to prevent their release to, or use by, customers, competitors, suppliers or distributors. However, it is worth noting that is not always necessary to be overly protectionist; third parties may not be able to use those intellectual assets they gain access to in circumstances where such use would require a record of the asset's pedigree, an understanding of

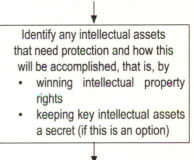

Identify any intellectual assets that need protection and how this will be accomplished, that is, by
- winning intellectual property rights
- keeping key intellectual assets a secret (if this is an option)

its limitations, supporting safety analysis, background data, and so on.

For those intellectual assets that do need to be protected the plan should, amongst other issues:

- Discuss the adequacy of existing management procedures and actions that are intended to prevent the disclosure, or transfer of, intellectual assets to third parties. If shortcomings are identified then improvements to these systems should be proposed. For instance, in the case of software, such procedures may require that source code is never released to third parties.

- Discuss whether the existing intellectual property rights, or those being sought, are sufficient to prevent undesirable third party use (the forms of intellectual property rights that are potentially available are discussed in Appendix 1). Here there may be benefit in running a brainstorming session at which technical, commercial and IP personnel try to find ways in which third parties could circumvent the existing protection. In the case of patents this type of exercise is often called patent busting.

- Identify what additional intellectual property rights (patents, trademarks and registered designs) need to be pursued, the territories that need to be covered, and the funding of such activities. For instance, in the case of trademarks this could discuss whether existing trademarks convey the right image for this offering, and hence whether new marks should be identified, cleared for use and registered.

- Where work is being subcontracted, or carried out by contract staff, the intellectual asset plan should consider what actions can, and should, be taken to minimize their freedom to exploit existing and arising intellectual assets. If no action is possible then the plan should seek to quantify the risks resulting from this inability to control such access.

- Discuss whether the experimental work is likely to yield the type of information needed to support any patent applications.

The intellectual asset plan should also discuss whether intellectual property rights are needed for strategic reasons. Specifically, intellectual property rights may be needed:

- as a basis of a licence to generate revenue, gain access to third party's intellectual property in a cross license, establish a technology as an industry standard, share risks and uncertainties, to provide for faster/ wider market entry, and so on;
- to create added value in a planned flotation;
- to make the organization a more attractive teaming or joint venture partner.

Exporting know-how

If the project will generate know-how of generic use across the organization then this should be highlighted. The plan should then identify those actions necessary to ensure its capture and dissemination either as a capability summary, or as input into a Community of Practice, and so on.

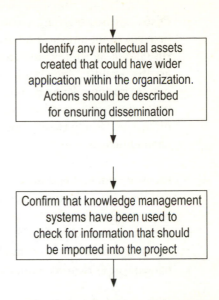

Importing know-how

The intellectual asset plan should also confirm that checks have been made, using appropriate knowledge management systems, for data or best practice that should be imported into the project. Where this has already taken place then a commentary on the strengths and weaknesses of such assets should be made and passed to those charged with updating the organization's intellectual asset strategy and knowledge map. If relevant know-how has been identified then confirmation should also be given that it has been, or will be, imported into the project.

Ongoing access

The intellectual asset plan should further consider whether any action is necessary to secure the ongoing availability of key intellectual assets. Specifically:

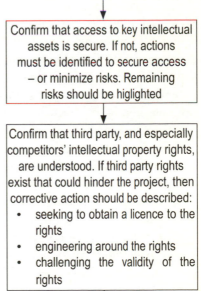

- Could third parties have, or win, intellectual property rights that would prevent the use of these intellectual assets? If third party rights are identified, restricting the use of technology to be deployed by the project, then one of the following options will need to be proposed: adopting an alternative technical solution, seeking a licence from the right holder, or challenging the validity of the rights (assuming there are grounds to mount such action).

- Could access to key intellectual assets be lost? Scenarios that need to be considered are the loss of key internal expertise, the loss of access to externally sourced capabilities, and so on.

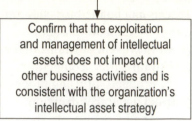

Confirm that the exploitation and management of intellectual assets does not impact on other business activities and is consistent with the organization's intellectual asset strategy

In all cases the plan should describe the actions being taken to quantify and minimize the risks of losing access. Actions could include:

- conducting searches for third party patents;
- rotating jobholders to ensure key skills are duplicated;
- carrying out "patent busting" reviews of third party patents.

Interaction between plans

The project should confirm that its use, protection, maintenance, capture and sharing of intellectual assets is consistent with the organization's intellectual asset strategy. It is also advisable to confirm, if possible, that the project's use of intellectual assets will not have a detrimental impact on the organization's wider activities.

PATENT PLANS

Just because an invention is patentable does not necessarily mean a patent should be sought. Each business area or project will need to consider whether patenting is the best way of securing market position. There are a number of options:

- Keep the information secret. Patenting by its nature involves the release of information into the public domain and an organization may judge that it is preferable to keep the invention secret – even though this runs the risk that a third party may file a patent first.
- Publish the information. This action will ensure that another organization cannot gain a patent. This of course will prevent the inventing organization from gaining a patent – but it has the advantage of being a low cost option.
- Seek a patent.

Patents can be filed for one, or more, reasons:

- to prevent others from copying products or processes;
- to restrict competitors' freedoms, by stopping them introducing products, or using processes, even if the patent holder has no intention of using the invention;
- as advertising – to show activity in particular areas;
- as an asset in teaming, licensing or disposals.

There are a number of terms used to describe the type of patent protection organizations will seek; Glazier[1] and Jackson-Knight[2] use the terms 'picket fence' and 'toll gate' patenting strategies. A picket fence strategy involves the generation of a series of patents capturing incremental improvements filed either around your own, or others' patents. As the technology and market evolves then these may become more important than the original or 'base' patent. A toll gate strategy involves extrapolating from current data to identify future developments which are then covered by speculative patent filings. If such a trend can be determined and a patent won, then any such patent may stop competitors from deploying the results of future research.

When a decision has been made to file a patent, then the timing of any application will need to be carefully considered; here there are three pressures. Firstly, an organization may fear that its competitors may file their own patent and deny it access to the market. Secondly, filing a patent involves information being released into the public domain and this will alert competitors. Thirdly, it is important that there is sufficient technical information to support and substantiate the patent application; if this is not available then it may be necessary to delay the application while development work continues. The decision on when to patent is therefore often a difficult one. There are perhaps two key questions to ask in determining which option should be taken.

1   Glazier, S. *Patent Strategies for Business*, London: Euromoney Publications, 1995.
2   Jackson-Knight, H. *Patent Strategy for Researchers and Research Managers*, Chichester: Wiley, 1996.

- How strong is the prior art[3] in this area? If there is little then early filing may give you a particularly strong patent and hence your competitors may be unable to react even if they are alerted.
- How likely is it that other organizations could be working in the field and hence file a blocking patent?

Territorial coverage will also need to be considered; in many cases it will not be necessary to file a patent in all the markets an organization wishes to pursue. For instance if the cost of third parties' entering the market is high, and there a limited number of key markets, it may only be necessary to have patent protection in these key markets. This limited filing program may block access to a sufficiently high proportion of the market to make it uneconomic for a competitor to pursue the smaller market sectors, even if they remain open. On the question of filing territories, Helfgott[4] lists six specific grounds for foreign filings:

- Protect local manufacture.
- Cover competitors' home countries or major investment/manufacturing countries.
- Cover major markets.
- Cover export sales.
- Cover those nations in which the product is likely to be copied.
- Cover the nations with anticipated commercial use.

The rate at which technology is evolving is another variable which must be considered when deciding whether to seek patent protection. In some markets, the delay between the invention being made and its introduction is sometimes so long that commercialization will only take place after the patent protection has run out. Conversely, in other industries it may not be possible to win patent protection before the product's life cycle has been completed.

Figure 12.2 seeks to summarize the issues that need to be considered in developing a patenting plan.

---

3   Prior art is a term used to describe the totality of the information published on a particular area. This represents the area that cannot be patented because it can no longer be regarded as novel.
4   Helfgott, S., Berman, C. *Global Intellectual Property Series 1992: Practical Strategies – Patent*, New York, NY: Practising Law Institute, 1992.

Topic	Issue
Do patents have a role in creating or preserving a monopoly/market lead?	Are patents critical in securing market edge or can the business survive without them? Is secrecy or publication a better option than patenting?
When should patents be pursued?	Should the patent be filed quickly or is the market such that the risk of another organization filing is slight?
Which are the key countries to file in?	Which countries need to be denied to the competition in order to make the market unattractive to them?
How strong is the patent coverage likely to be won?	How much prior art exists? Are the patents being filed as improvements over existing technology, or a totally new process where the patent being sought is likely to provide a strong monopoly?
How rapidly is the area evolving and are the initial patents likely to provide the protection when needed?	How long is the product or service likely to be saleable? Does this match with the life span of protection being granted by a patent?
A cost benefit analysis	What additional profit margin are the patents likely to give? Specifically, what are the likely patenting costs and can they be justified?

Figure 12.2   Challenges facing patent decision making

SOFTWARE PLANS

The protection of software is concerned with three issues:

- protection of the source code;
- protection of the appearance and structure of the software, including the user interface;
- prevention of unauthorized copying, distribution and use of the compiled code.

The legal position is often complex and the rights available are not always clear cut. Further, while decompilation and reverse engineering are often prohibited by software license agreements this will not always stop an unscrupulous competitor, or an enthusiastic hacker from analysing computer code. As a consequence it is better to use good housekeeping to prevent or hinder copying – rather than being in a position to have to take legal action after copying has taken place.

Examples of good management practice:

- Understand what IP is most commercially sensitive – programme structure, equations, data and so on, and then make life difficult for those who may wish to copy it by:
  – restricting access to flow charts;
  – removing comments from source code, or even adding misleading ones;
  – avoiding putting too much information in manuals;
  – changing the structure of the code to make it difficult for others to understand its internal operation;
  – changing the names of local and member variables in the code to hide their function. Decompilers therefore have less information on which to base their analysis, and it becomes harder for programmers to understand any code they are analysing.
- Don't overlook basic security – minimize contractors' access to trade secrets, keep commercially sensitive material in locked cabinets, and so on.
- Manage trade secrets in a manner commensurate with their importance, and be able to demonstrate that such care has been taken. e.g.: using labelling where appropriate to highlight any information that is commercially sensitive. This may become important if an organization ever has to prove those receiving commercially sensitive information were aware of its sensitivity.
- Ensuring computer code generates a copyright statement on the computer screen and on printouts. Copyright statements should also be visible on computer disks, manuals, and so on.
- Use of digital watermarks. Watermarking can uniquely mark every distributed copy of a software product. If an illegitimate copy of a piece of software is discovered, the mark allows for unambiguous identification of the source of piracy. This application of watermarking is often termed "fingerprinting".

BRANDING PLANS

Freedom for use

Selecting a new brand can be a long and expensive affair; not only must the chosen brand convey the right image, but it must also be available for use. When choosing a new brand, an organization will normally short list half a dozen or more acceptable brands that it would be willing to use, and then carry out a detailed check to establish which, if any, are free for use. This process of clearance must not only seek identical brands, but also those that either look or sound similar. This search will involve a study of trademark registrations, company names, Internet domain names and general Internet searches.

These searches will arguably need to be carried out in all the territories where the brand is likely to be used. However, in an effort to control costs, which can be significant, it is usual to carry out these national reviews in series rather than parallel. This clearly takes longer, but will enable the number of brands reviewed to be trimmed as conflicting trademarks are identified, and brands discarded as the searches continue.

Where an identical trademark is found to be already in use, or registered, by an organization selling similar products or services, then use of the new brand is clearly inadvisable and potentially infringing. In cases where the trademarks are similar, but the products/services are not identical then it may be possible to proceed with the brand. However, if the difference is slight then it would be wise to seek consent from the holder of the existing rights. It is common for the right holder to seek financial compensation for granting such consent; and such payments may be significant if the organization seeking consent is large and has already committed itself to use of this trademark.

The right form of protection

When deciding what brands to protect via registration, it is important to understand the trademark's role. Trademarks can be filed not only to stop competitors and counterfeiters using your brand but also to:

- help check whether the trademark is available (as the process of registration includes a search for existing, conflicting, third party rights);

- to provide an asset that can be licensed to third parties or group companies;
- to stop the brand being misused by protesters, campaign groups, and so on;
- to demonstrate commercial use of the name if it becomes necessary to evict "cyber squatters" who have registered a domain name with no intention of using it, but instead in the hope of reselling it, at an unrealistic price, to an organization wishing to use the name.

However, it is important to recognize that a trademark does not need to be registered before it can be used. This is discussed in Appendix 1.

Unlike most jurisdictions, in the EU a trademark can be protected as a Registered Design. This is a low cost option, and in certain circumstances may provide stronger protection than that afforded by a trademark. However, the design must be novel to be registered, so it is important that such registration is considered early in the marketing strategy.

Watching how your trademark is being used

If your goods are liable to counterfeiting then to prevent loss of sales, and damage to your reputation, it is important that the market is monitored for unauthorized use of the trademark. This clearly requires a good understanding of what is happening in the market, and clear lines of internal reporting, so that problems can be highlighted and appropriately managed. This can be augmented by the use of image recognition software that can scan the Internet to search for occasions where your brand is being corrupted or misused.

It is also important to ensure that your brand does not become so successful that it starts to be used as a generic description. If this happens then there is a danger that the trademark may be declared invalid, as trademarks cannot be used to protect descriptive names. Trademarks that have become victims to this problem, and hence been rendered invalid, include: elevator, cellophane, aspirin, escalator, gramophone, linoleum and thermos.

Trademark revocation is therefore a considerable risk if a marketing strategy encourages customers to start using a trademark as a generic term for a product type. Many organizations understand the risk this possesses and provide guidelines on how their trademark is to be used, both within the organization and to third parties. Action should be taken when the trademark is used by third parties as a generic description or where the ™ or ® symbols are not used. While it is not possible to force others to use trademarks in specific ways, if a trademark's owner has taken all reasonable steps in explaining to third parties how the trademark should be used, then this is likely to be taken into account if the courts ever consider its validity. However, taking such action against trademark misuse is clearly an expensive option.

Reviewing protection

Routine checks should be made to ensure that any protection in place continues to match the business's need. Regular reviews should therefore be carried out to check that the trademark plan is up to date by reviewing whether:

- the importance of any unregistered marks has increased to the point where registration is justified;
- the use of a registered mark has been extended into new territories;
- the appearance of any trademark has evolved sufficiently to be outside the scope of the original filing;
- third parties have not filed conflicting marks that could, if granted, lead to the dilution of your rights. (This activity is normally carried out by computer watching services looking for published applications in official trademark gazettes and directories.);
- that the trademarks have not become vulnerable to revocation because of a lack of commercial use.

If an organization makes use of a post launch Stage-Gate process then criteria can be added to ensure the above reviews are triggered; reminders can also be entered in the diary systems used by patent and trademark attorneys to manage their workflow.

INTELLECTUAL ASSET PLANS – IN CONCLUSION

As has been seen above, an intellectual asset plan can range from the simple to the complex. It should also be stressed that intellectual asset plans are living documents that evolve as the project, product or service they support evolves. Initially they will identify actions and uncertainties, but ultimately will do no more than review and monitor the adequacy of actions already taken. Further, the relative importance of each form of intellectual asset and intellectual property right can change during the life of a product or service.

For instance, in the pharmaceutical industry, a drug's key intellectual assets will initially be in the form of know-how and proprietary information that will be protected by secrecy or confidentiality. A patent may then be obtained preventing others from producing a generic equivalent. When the patent expires, a trademark may then become critical in securing ongoing sales in a market where there is likely to be cheaper generic substitutes available.

CHAPTER 13

IA MANAGEMENT WITHIN A GROUP OF COMPANIES

If there is an overlap, either between the markets different group companies are exploiting, or the technologies they are deploying, then the challenges facing intellectual asset management will increase significantly. In this scenario, not only must decision-making take into account the often conflicting needs of multiple companies, but further, if the collective intellectual asset portfolio is to be effectively leveraged then it must be visible and accessible to all group members.

While intellectual asset management may be more complex than in a single company, the tools described previously, and shown in Figure 13.1, can be readily adapted to service the needs of a group.

Figure 13.1 The six facets of integrated intellectual asset management

- Decision-making bodies and systems must ensure that, where appropriate, group companies are consulted and involved in decision making. For example, projects and services should be required to identify instances where they are sharing intellectual assets with group companies, both to ensure intra group agreements are put in place and also to enable management to build up a picture of those capabilities that are important across the group.

- The quality of intellectual asset management in each group company must be monitored and challenged. For example, intellectual asset management in a group of companies is often only as strong as the weakest link, so it is important that best practice is shared and weakness highlighted.

- The policy and accountability framework should be expanded to identify the actions each subsidiary should undertake, as well as those residing at group level. For example, should a single person, or body, be nominated to review and sanction all intellectual asset licenses or abandonments.

- Individuals within all group companies must be helped to understand their role in the management and protection of the group's intellectual assets.

- For capabilities that are being exploited by more than one group company, then an intellectual asset strategy should exist to guide decision making within all companies.

- Detailed management processes must be developed by group companies, that work seamlessly with the initiatives described above, to manage a group's knowledge, information, patents, trademarks, and so on.

However, outside of these areas, there are two challenges that are unique to the management of intellectual assets within a group of companies, specifically:

- Where intellectual assets are being shared amongst group companies, then intra-group agreements will be needed to define the roles of each company. That is, the allocation of risks arising from the intellectual

asset's exploitation, how the returns are to be allocated, who will own any improvements, and so on.
- In many instances transfer pricing[1] legislation forces the members of a group of companies to charge each other an arms-length price (that is, the price the IP would be licensed or sold for in an open market) for access to each other's goods and services, including intellectual assets.

The following sections consider these challenges.

OWNERSHIP

A group will need to review and decide how to structure the ownership of its intellectual assets. There are five basic models that can be followed, each with advantages and disadvantages:

- Corporate ownership, in which the intellectual assets are owned and managed at the group level.
- Ownership by a single existing group company.
- Distributed ownership where each group company owns those intellectual assets underpinning its business activities.
- Co-ownership where each group company is given an equal share in the title to all, or a proportion of, the intellectual asset portfolio.
- Ownership by a company formed solely for the purpose of managing and exploiting the group's intellectual assets portfolio.

This last model can reduce the group's overall tax exposure if the resulting intragroup licences are used to repatriate profits to a holding company based in a low tax regime. It should also be noted that where there is a significant intra-group trade in intellectual property then the creation of a dedicated IP

---

1   Transfer pricing legislation has been introduced, by tax authorities worldwide, to prevent groups of companies from using intra-group agreements to repatriate their profits to off-shore tax havens. Without such legislation, it would be possible for each member of a group of companies to sell its intellectual property, for a nominal sum, to a subsidiary based in a low tax regime. This subsidiary could then license this intellectual property back to other group companies at a grossly inflated royalty rate. In the extreme this practice would mean that the only member of the group making a profit would be the company based in a tax haven. Tax authorities are able to stop such tax avoidance by forcing members of the same group to charge an arms-length price for any transfers of, or access to, intellectual property. However, the requirement on companies to demonstrate that each transaction is at an arms-length rate is a significant bureaucratic overhead.

holding company may be justified as a method of simplifying the bureaucracy that is created by the need to comply with transfer pricing legislation.

However, when deciding on an ownership model, the first and most important question is: which structure will be the most effective at managing, and ensuring the full exploitation of, the organization's intellectual assets? If there are several equally valid approaches then the model that yields the greatest financial savings advantage should clearly be adopted.

The choice of ownership structure will therefore be driven by issues such as:

- Are intellectual assets a common resource, accessed by several companies, where central ownership will help ensure management's focus will be on the needs of the group as a whole?
- Are each company's markets and/or technologies independent, with little opportunity or need for cross-licensing intellectual assets between group companies?
- Are there significant external, non-core, licensing opportunities that are likely to be overlooked if intellectual assets are owned by individual group companies following narrowly focused business plans?
- Is the group's business strategy supported – or should it be supported – by licensing, either to third parties or partners; and further, are there instances where the granting of such licenses, while in the interests of the group, would be resisted by individual businesses?
- Does each business fund its own R&D, or is R&D centralized with perhaps joint funding of certain projects? (Central ownership of intellectual assets is easier to achieve if the activities generating these assets are centrally funded.)
- Which is the simplest model to administer?
- Are there likely to be future changes in the group structure, such as sales, flotations or joint ventures, which would be easier to manage if intellectual assets were owned by individual companies?
- Can tax breaks be won by centralizing intellectual asset ownership in a dedicated holding company based in a low tax regime?

Given the complex nature of many multinationals, the answers to these questions are unlikely to provide a unique solution to intellectual asset ownership. A group may therefore adopt a mixed approach, for example, where intellectual assets are co-owned when they relate to a technology that underpins several businesses, while as a default intellectual assets are owned by whichever company they most directly support.

Ownership by a holding company

The formation of a central holding company is likely to be attractive if:

* the group's intellectual assets can be regarded as a common resource accessed by several companies.;
* there are significant unrealized external licensing opportunities that could be pursued by a holding company able to focus on the pursuit of such opportunities;
* such an ownership structure can generate significant ongoing tax savings, or minimize the bureaucracy associated with complying with transfer price legislation.

However, before a decision is made to pursue this option, the disadvantages need to be considered:

* The formation of a holding company implies a transfer of control and accountabilities. For instance, placing the ownership of a brand with a holding company implies that elements of the marketing strategy will be run centrally with a global perspective – this may represent a benefit, or risk, depending on the nature of the business.
* Any pre-existing intellectual assets that are to be transferred between tax jurisdictions will need to be identified, valued and sold to the holding company. This is in itself a significant, costly, undertaking.
* In general the holding company will need to pay for the maintenance of its intellectual assets, using the licence fees it receives from third parties and other group companies. As a result the holding company will need robust decision-making processes to ensure that cost-bearing decisions are business driven.

Considering these issues in more detail:

Control and accountabilities

Central ownership implies central control, or at least co-ordination, and this often runs counter to the decentralized operation of many groups. Systems can clearly be put in place to ensure that the requirements of other group companies are visible, but the holding company will ultimately need to take many decisions, including which patents to maintain and which to abandon.

Transfer of ownership

Where a group decides it should centralize ownership then it will clearly be necessary to arrange for the transfer of title of these assets to the holding company. If this involves the transfer of assets between tax jurisdictions then both to comply with transfer pricing legislation, and to win any available tax breaks, the transfer of these intellectual assets will need to take place at an arms-length price – which means that the transferred assets will need to be identified, valued, purchased and the change of ownership registered. This can be a major undertaking.

Further, if new intellectual assets are continually being developed then a mechanism will need to be developed to centralize ownership of these assets, again on an arms-length basis. One way in which this transfer can be affected is if the holding company pays for some, or all of, the organization's R&D. In this instance, the holding company will extract a licence income from each group company for the use of the intellectual assets it already owns; this is then used to fund the R&D, and hence automatically gain ownership of the arising intellectual assets. However, this approach will only work if the majority of the organization's intellectual assets are derived from R&D expenditure.

If the group wishes to obtain licences to third party IPRs then it may be appropriate for the holding company to be the licensee, onward licensing these rights on to relevant group companies. The role of the holding company can be further extended so that it manages the licences historically obtained from third parties; in this case the original agreements will need to be reviewed to see if they allow the necessary transfers and internal licensing.

Expenditure and income

To preserve any tax breaks created by the formation of a holding company, the commercial arrangements struck with the rest of the group must be arms length. This will apply to the following transactions:

- The costs associated with maintaining the intellectual asset portfolio.
- The costs associated with obtaining new intellectual assets – either from third parties or other group companies.
- The licensing of intellectual assets to group companies.

These are best considered according to the type of intellectual asset being held.

CENTRAL OWNERSHIP OF TRADEMARKS

At first sight, registering any new trademarks in the name of a holding company, based in a low tax regime, would appear to be a simple way of minimizing a group's tax burden. The initial value of the brand will be nominal and this would be reflected in the holding company's initial investment. However, once established the brand is likely to generate sizeable royalty streams from other group companies and hence succeed in repatriating profits to a low tax regime.

Unfortunately, unless the holding company is paying for advertising and marketing, then the value of the brand will not be increased by its actions, so it is demonstrably not an arms-length relationship for it to gain an income from the use of the enhanced brand.

The holding company must therefore not only to pay for marketing, but also have control of the brand's use. Placing ownership of the brand with a holding company is therefore not without risks; but this form of centralized control can on occasion be an attractive proposition, in which an income stream is generated by licensing that can then be used to promote and develop brands. However, it is important that the intra-group agreements allow both the holding company, and its licensees, the freedoms they need to maximize returns to the group. Responsibilities therefore need to be clearly defined, for example:

- The holding company can be charged with running global licensing, advertising and sponsorship activities, together with registering trademarks and setting guidelines governing the use and appearance of the brand. This imposition of a consistent brand appearance, and brand development strategy, can be one of the principal justifications driving the formation of a holding company.
- The internal licensees can be charged with the control of local advertising, promotions and sponsorships.

Clearly, the ongoing royalty arrangements will need to be structured to reflect the role, risks, returns and investments of each party.

CENTRAL OWNERSHIP OF PATENTS

Here any existing patents will again need to be acquired by the holding company at an arms-length price. Further, if arising patents are also to be acquired then either the holding company will need to sponsor the R&D generating the patents, or purchase any patents at an arms-length price.

The holding company will also need to use its license income to fund the ongoing prosecution and maintenance of its patent portfolio. These patenting costs can be significant and in general the license fee charged to the businesses will not increase according to the expenditure on patents. This may encourage individual group companies to lobby for the filing and maintenance of new IPRs, even in circumstances where the business case for such action is weak. The holding company will therefore need to have access to personnel who have a clear understanding of what patents are, and are not, required by group companies to ensure the patent portfolio represents good value for money.

CENTRAL OWNERSHIP OF METHODS AND DATA

It is relatively unusual to transfer ownership of this type of intellectual asset to a holding company. However, here again there may be commercial or tax benefits that accrue from centralized ownership.

As is the case with trademarks there are generally ongoing costs that are necessary to maintain, or enhance, the value of these intellectual assets. Specifically, methods and data evolve over time and the ownership of these improvements must be acquired by the holding company as part of an arms-length relationship. This clearly must involve the holding company either purchasing these new intellectual assets, or contributing to the cost of making the improvements. One way in which this can be achieved is to structure the licence so that the holding company acquires ownership of these improvements for a sum that is deducted from the royalty stream it receives for access to the existing methods and data.

TAX BENEFITS

The type of intra-group licensing discussed here can, on occasion, be structured to minimize a group's tax burden by using the licences to repatriate profit to a holding company based in a low tax regime. However, to avoid falling foul of anti-avoidance rules the centralization of IP ownership must be driven by a commercial need, rather than the desire to minimize tax payments. These could include:

- the benefit of central control and co-ordination of brand use and development;
- the need to pursue external non-core licensing opportunities, which would otherwise be overlooked by the existing businesses;
- the need to minimize bureaucracy arising from existing intra-border trade in IP.

Even where there is a business case for the transfer of assets, the tax authorities may challenge the transactions on any one of a number of grounds. For instance, in the case of trademarks it is a general principle that goodwill cannot be separated, and transferred independently, from other business assets. Therefore it may be argued that the value of any transferred trademark is very much less than the value of the brand as a whole.

PRACTICAL ASPECTS OF INTRA-GROUP LICENSING

Intra-group agreements

Whenever intellectual assets are being shared amongst group companies it is generally necessary to put in place a series of enabling agreements to satisfy transfer pricing legislation. However, even where these agreements are not required by transfer pricing concerns, their use is good practice as they ensure each party understands their rights and responsibilities.

Sometimes it is possible to put in place one or more high-level licences granting access to all of a licensor's intellectual assets for an defined annual fee. However, often these enabling licences will have to be technology or opportunity specific. The negotiation of these intra-group agreements can be extremely time consuming, and on occasion more problematic than between unrelated entities. These difficulties are caused by several pressures:

- When companies are part of the same group, the licensee may expect to be granted a licence on preferential terms. In reality there will be many reasons, including transfer price legislation, which will persuade licensors to pursue an arms-length relationship in these internal negotiations. The gap between licensees' and licensors' expectations may therefore, on occasion, be greater than is the case between unrelated entities.

• Licensees may regard the agreement of an internal licence as a low priority, purely procedural issue, which can be dealt with when time permits. There is therefore a danger that contracts with third parties, which provide access to other group company's intellectual assets, may be pursued or even closed, without first putting in place an enabling intra-group agreement. This can cause enormous problems where an agreement is struck with a third party that has flow-down provisions which are unacceptable to the group company that owns the intellectual asset.

• Negotiations involving a third party are normally subject to time constraints that force both parties to make compromises and concessions. When the negotiations are intra-group, there are likely to be internal politics that will ensure external business opportunities are not missed, even if an internal intra-group licence is not in place. Without time constraints intransigent negotiating positions can be adopted by both sides.

• Where there is a good working relationship between the technical or commercial communities in group companies, there is likely to be an exchange of intellectual assets that is invisible to management. While in some ways this open access is beneficial, it can given rise to liabilities that can on occasion outweigh the benefits of such open exchange.

Where there is a significant intra-group trade in intellectual assets, time and effort will be saved by developing standard licences, methods of valuing intellectual assets, and even a policy defining the default terms for the intra-group trade in intellectual assets. Such a policy will need to address the following issues:

• The allocation of risks, such as those that arising from product liability and the infringement of third party rights.
• Whether the licensee should take action to identify, quantify or lay-off risks.
• At what point in the product, or bid, pipeline should a formal intra-group licence be put in place.

- Who is responsible for approving intra-group licences, changes to standard terms, and the release of information to third parties?
- Who is responsible for granting third parties access to both existing, and arising, group intellectual assets?
- How should the ownership, and rights to, arising intellectual assets be distributed within the group?

With more complex group structures it will also be necessary to decide how to cascade licensed rights down to subsidiaries of subsidiaries. For instance, if all intellectual assets are owned by a single subsidiary, should that company be able to license all group companies directly as shown in Figure 13.2, or should licensing only take place along the reporting structure.

An ability to license all group companies directly will minimize the number of licences. However, this may be resisted as it can be perceived as by-passing normal managerial controls and reporting structures. Further, more flexibility is available if licences follow the ownership structure, as this preserves the option of changing some of the licence terms, such as the allocation of risks and costs, which are cascaded down at each organizational level.

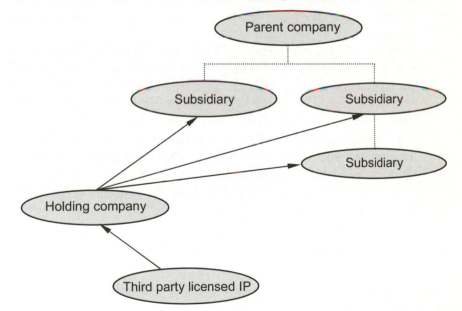

Figure 13.2 Internal licensing of intellectual assets by-passing normal managerial controls

Internal controls and approvals

Clearly an organization will not wish to introduce barriers, or bureaucracy, that unnecessarily hinder the sharing and exploitation of the collective intellectual asset portfolio. However, some controls are clearly necessary, for example to ensure that:

- trade secrets are not disseminated too widely, or passed on to third parties without necessary approvals;
- transfers of intellectual assets are monitored so that matching transfer price compliant agreements can be put in place.

Conversely, it is clearly inefficient to put in place an opportunity-specific intra-group licence until it is clear that the intellectual assets in question will actually be used. An organization will therefore need to decide at what point transfers should be formally recorded, sanctioned and licensed, and when transfers can proceed without approvals. For instance, it may be decided that:

- transfers of non-proprietary information, for internal review and evaluation, can take place against a generic intra-group confidentiality agreement;
- transfers of non-proprietary information needed to support the preparation of a bid (where at the time of transfer it is uncertain whether the intellectual assets will be commercially exploited) can take place, provided it is agreed, during bid preparation, that the default terms for intra-group trade are acceptable if the contract is won;
- if the anticipated use would require a variation in the standard terms for intra-group trade, then it may be appropriate to insist that the licence terms are agreed before transfer takes place;
- once it is clear that commercial exploitation will take place then a formal agreement should be put in place.

This type of control system is shown in Figure 13.3.

Clearly it is desirable to minimize the number of agreements that need to be put in place:

	Transfer takes place against a generic non-disclosure agreement	Transfer takes place subject to confirmation that the standard terms for intra-group trading are acceptable	Transfer takes place against a formalized licence
Transfer of non-proprietary information for internal review	✓		
Transfer of proprietary information for internal review		✓	
Bid preparation and submission		✓	
Commercial work			✓

Figure 13.3   Sanctioning the transfer of intellectual assets

- If the exchanges will lead to the improvement of business systems, such as safety protocols, then it may be appropriate to put in place a one-off overarching agreement covering all transfers and uses.
- If the transfers will only lead to the creation of large one-off opportunities then it is probably appropriate to put in place a proforma agreement each time an opportunity is realized.
- If there are numerous, low value, ad-hoc exchanges then it may be appropriate to put in place a one-off agreement that seeks to capture the generic responsibilities, roles and the allocation of risks.

It is clearly important that when an agreement is put in place it matches the true nature of the relationship, for example:

- Is the agreement a simple licence?
- Are risks or costs being shared; if so it may be necessary to put in place a collaboration agreement rather than a licence?
- If both licensee and licensor are sharing the results of parallel development work then the relationship may be more appropriately represented by a teaming agreement.

It is often easier to correctly characterize an organization's relationship with a third party. When putting in place an agreement with a group company it can be more difficult to recognize the true relationship; for instance, a partnership can easily be misrepresented as a licence, if the true extent of the party's interdependence is not recognized.

Assisting transfers

It is also important to consider introducing systems that can aid in the transfer of technology between individual companies:

- "Experts" can be nominated who are able to field technical or commercial enquiries from other group companies (this is explored below).
- Once opportunities have been identified that require the transfer of technology then it may be appropriate to develop a formal plan identifying key actions, as described below.
- Decision-making processes can be used to ensure that all projects are reviewed to establish if they are importing or exporting intellectual assets to group companies. This has already been discussed in Chapter 5.
- Information on inventions can be disseminated, in part, by ensuring key group companies are represented on any patent committee. This is an aspect of patent management and was addressed in Chapter 10.
- It may be appropriate to record the flow of information so that updates, or errors, in passed drawings/papers are highlighted.

The experts described above can be used to raise the visibility of, and assist in the transfer of, intellectual assets in targeted areas. Their role could therefore include:

- acting as a channel for initial enquiries into each group company's technical capabilities;
- where necessary, developing plans to facilitate the transfer of intellectual assets;
- acting to clear and log the release of information required to facilitate the above.

Once an opportunity has been identified for transferring and exploiting intellectual assets amongst group companies, it may also be appropriate for such individuals to develop plans that:

- Identify all the intellectual assets that will be required during the commercialization of the technology, and decide whether they will be transferred, duplicated or retained.
- Identify any skills or knowledge that will be needed to commercialize the technology, and describe how any skills gaps are to be filled. If this is via staff secondment or transfer from other group companies, then individuals will need to be identified and the consequences of such transfer planned for – including the time taken for any necessary visa applications. Alternatively, if staff are to be trained, then the time this takes must be included in the plan.
- Assess whether the existing IPRs are adequate for the new market.
- Describe where raw materials or subcomponents should be sourced.

Design standards are of particular concern in the engineering environment. Different countries have different design standards; an example would be design criteria for pressure vessels. Designs, or methods, may therefore need to be updated before technology can be used by another group company.

It may also be appropriate for both companies to work together to identify the key messages that are to be given during the marketing of the technology in the new market. This can be used to establish a theme for conferences, bid documents, advertising material, and so on.

CHAPTER 14

LICENSING

LICENSING STRATEGY

Historically, many organizations have been reluctant to systematically out-license their core technologies and brands. This, sometimes blinkered, strategy often stems from a fear that licensing could increase competitive pressures in core markets, or to the devaluing of brands, and hence ultimately a reduction in profitability.

However, a growing number of organizations have found that licensing not only enables them to exploit non-core markets, but also, on occasion, to achieve a better balance between risks and returns from their core markets.

A few companies have been able to generate significant revenue through the licensing of their IP portfolio; these include the following.[1]

	Estimated annual earnings from IP US$ millions
IBM	1,500
Qualcomm	800
Thomson	500
Lucent Technologies	500
DuPont	450

---

1   Joff Wild, 'Are Your Rights Going to Work?', *IPReview*, Issue 7, Computer Patent Annuities Limited Partnership, 2004; J.R. Sobieraj, 'Current Issues and Future Trends for Large Corporate Licensing Programs', *Les Nouvelles*, June 2004.

The success of such companies has led many organizations to believe that, hidden in their portfolio is overlooked IP that can, and should, be used to generate licence income. However, experience shows that licensing is not about mining the portfolio for under-exploited IP, but instead about finding new ways of generating income from IP that is already an important part of the organization's business.

It should also be recognized that licensing can be undertaken for a number of reasons in addition to simple revenue generation:

- Some organizations develop and hold IP portfolios principally to avoid litigation; this strategy is followed by companies such as GE and Sun Microsystems. In these markets the patent landscape is often so complicated that it is extremely difficult to avoid infringing patents – as this is an equally intractable problem for all competitors in this sector, most are willing to license or cross-license IP to avoid litigation.[2]
- In other instances the IP portfolio can be used to generate value by establishing partnerships with customers, suppliers and distributors; this strategy is followed by Microsoft, P&G, HP and Dow Chemicals.[3]
- Finally, some organizations have found that licensing enables them to exploit non-core markets that would otherwise be inaccessible. This strategy is followed by Boeing, Lucent Technologies, IBM and BellSouth. In addition companies such as Coca-Cola and Harley-Davidson follow this route to extract revenue from their brands.[4]

An organization should therefore proactively identify those combinations of patents, brands, know-how and markets that can be exploited via licensing, and those that are to be exploited solely via the sale of products or services. In the extreme an organization may reverse the normal business model and decide that licensing should only be prohibited in the case of specifically identified technologies, brands and markets; outside of these areas licensees should be pursued, even if this creates competition for the organization's existing products and services. Therefore as part of its intellectual asset strategy an organization may decide to:

---

2   Harrison, S. 'From Sunk Costs to Sound Strategies', *IP Review*, Issue 7, Computer Patenting Annuities Limited Partnership, 2004.
3   Ibid.
4   Ibid.

- license IP to competitors, suppliers, distributors or customers where this represents a better balance between risks and returns;
- withdraw from certain markets in instances where the sale of enabled products and services is diverting the organization's financial, managerial or technical resources from core, or more valuable, opportunities; and instead license the technology;
- set up an internal incubator able to assist in the creation of start-up companies where there are no obvious external licensees, and the opportunity cannot be effectively leveraged by the organization's existing businesses;
- establish joint ventures, or other relationships, with third parties better placed to exploit identified market opportunities.

A LICENSING FUNCTION

Where licensing has a significant role to play within an organization's business plan, then the creation of a licensing function may be warranted. The process of identifying and pursuing licensees is time consuming, and unless a dedicated resource is available such activities may not get the priority and resources needed. Hence without a licensing function, licensing will often become reactive, responding to requests from potential licensors or to short-lived management initiatives. Further, licensing is a demanding, challenging activity and those involved need specialist skills.

The pressure to create a licensing function generally builds with time, as an organization gradually develops a belief that licensing is a core activity. Such a licensing function will typically be a corporate profit centre, thus ensuring its independence from the operational businesses. As a profit centre there may be merit in this function funding some, or all, of the organization's patent prosecution.

In certain circumstances it may be more attractive for an organization to create an IP holding company to deal with licensing, rather than a licensing function. As was discussed in Chapter 13 this may also enable the organization to either realize tax savings, or minimize the bureaucracy necessary to comply with transfer price legislation.

A successful licensing function, or subsidiary, will not only need the ability to close agreements with potential licensees, but also identify licensing opportunities. This capability can only be built on good communications between the organization's legal, commercial and technical personnel. Specifically, such a network will need to understand:

- the IPRs their organization owns, and how these relate to those held by third parties;
- third party product groups and how they are developing;
- the technology areas where the organization has a market lead;
- the role of branding in the organization's core markets and an appreciation of those markets where the same brand promise and value are applicable.

Further, a licensing function will only prosper if due account is taken of the following points:

- Employees will need to be recruited with the experience and expertise necessary to understand the technology (or branding) landscape and negotiate what are often complex commercial agreements. This is a specialist skill-set.
- Licensors will need to be monitored, both to make sure they are using due diligence in exploiting the IP they have been licensed, and accurately reporting sales.
- A significant proportion of any licence income received should be reinvested to fund the identification of further licensees; it should not all be siphoned off to fund unrelated activities.
- The organization's licensing activities will need to be monitored with clear targets and benchmarking.

BRAND LICENSING

Only a few organizations manage to generate significant income by licensing their trademarks and brands. The limited licensing that does take place tends to be concentrated in the fashion and lifestyle markets, where some organizations are able to generate revenue from markets that would otherwise be inaccessible.

The low level of licensing is in part explained because the value of a brand, unlike other forms of intellectual property, can be reduced through misuse:

- Brands can clearly be damaged if they become associated with poor quality products or services, and hence licensors will exercise caution when seeking licensees.
- Brands can also be damaged if they are used in an inconsistent way in different market segments. Hence licensors will need to allocate time to specifying, and monitoring, how their brands are being used.

Licensing a brand therefore often involves the creation of a close working relationship between licensor and licensee. Indeed the licensor may be looking for a licensee with a similar culture- and value-set to its own. The licensor may also be looking for a licensee that is willing to develop and market products that are unique and superior so that they enhance, rather than reduce, the value of the brand.

Even where these difficulties can be managed, and a suitable licensee identified, only a few brands are amenable to licensing:

- The brand should not be closely associated with a unique product or service. In general only brands with an image that can be attached to a range of products or services are capable of generating significant licence income.
- Ideally the consumer must perceive the brand as implying a superior or high value offering, and hence be willing to select the product in preference to others.
- The target consumers must have a high awareness of the brand.
- The brand must be maintained – either through its continued use in the market, or through its ability to generate the revenue needed to fund advertising.

TECHNOLOGY LICENSING

Here IP is generally licensed to generate an income, but as has already been highlighted, this is not always the case. IP can be licensed for a range of reasons, for instance:

- in a cross license to end actual, or the risk of, litigation;
- as part of a joint venture, or other teaming arrangement;
- to share technology.

The signing of a technology licence can therefore mark the formation of a long-term co-operative relationship, the end of all correspondence, or a range of intermediate positions.

Identifying licensable technologies

The following sections seek to identify the main issues that need to be considered when deciding whether a given technology is suitable for licensing. If desired, these criteria can be developed to score, or rank, the licensability of technologies.

(1) Basics

- What products and services can be created or enhanced by the intellectual assets?
- What is their likely life span?
- What are the potential and likely volumes, net selling price (NSP) and margins?

(2) Acceptability to market

- Is this a solution to a visible market need, in other words, is this technology pull or push?
- Is the technology a significant advance on that already present in the market, and does this represent a strength or weakness?
- To what extent could the new offering be incorporated into existing products, or make use of existing production processes, in other words, what sunk investment is being leveraged?
- How mature is the market, and is this the optimum time to pursue the opportunity?
- Does the maturity of the technology, and status of the legal protection, match the market window?
- Will the legal protection afford a true, sustainable, monopoly and is there a risk that any IPRs could be challenged?

In summary, what are the chances of technology uptake at this time?

(3) What intellectual assets should be offered?

- Is the balance of added value in know-how or IPRs?

- Will the licensee need ongoing access to the licensor's know-how, and if so will it be available?
- Could there be a loss of the licensor's competitiveness resulting from the transfer of intellectual assets?
- Do third parties have intellectual assets that could be combined with the licensor's to make a more attractive offering?
- Could the licensing of these intellectual assets undermine other licensing opportunities?

In summary, what intellectual assets could, and should, be made available and what retained?

(4) Deal structure

- Could there be benefit in linking with another licensor to provide a more complete offering?
- Should an attempt be made to create an industry standard based on this technology (should licensees be offered exclusive or non-exclusive licenses)? If multiple licensees are to be sought, then to help establish the offering in the market place, is it appropriate to provide the first licensee with discounted royalty rates?
- Are there benefits in narrowly defining the rights granted to the licensees in order to segment the market by product, market or geography?
- In the case of a fragmented market is the licensor, or are potential licensees, best placed to grant further licences?
- Are all the routes for financial exposure understood, are they significant (what is the potential multiplier on the income stream), and can they be avoided or laid-off?
- Are improvements likely to be made by the licensees; if so does the licensor need to secure rights?
- Are improvements likely to be made by the licensor; if so should the licensees be granted rights?

In summary, what route offers the optimum balance of risks and returns for the licensor – pure licence, licence plus support, joint venture, start-up, cross licence, or strategic alliance?

Identifying licensees

The process of licensee identification should follow three steps. First, it is important to decide what type of organization is likely to be interested in the technology. Second, searches can be conducted to identify suitable licensees, and finally, the list of candidate organizations will need to be filtered.

(1) What are the ideal characteristics of a licensee (once identified these can be used to try to identify such organizations):

- Are there scarce capabilities that a licensee will need, other than those that could be provided by the licensor, to commercialize the product?
- How segmented is the market by technology, manufacturers, distributors, and so on, and hence are there few or many potential licensees?
- At what point in the supply chain should the technology be injected?
- Who, according to patent citation and competitor intelligence information, are the key players?
- Is there an opportunity, or benefit, in going outside of the existing supply/manufacturing/distribution chain?
- Could the technology cause a change in market dynamics that should be considered?
- Is there a danger of a challenge to the patent's validity that needs to be taken into account in identifying licensees?

In summary, what are the ideal characteristics of a licensee/partner, in terms of their distribution network, manufacturing base, visibility to customers, market presence, design and development capability, and so on.

(2) Potential licensees can be identified in a number of ways including:

- So-called "patent mining" can be carried out; this involves a review of third party patents to assess if the exploitation of the inventions described would infringe the licensor's patents. In recent years a number of software tools and consultants have appeared which can assist in this area.
- Organizations can purchase and examine third party products to ascertain if their patents are being infringed. Any infringers can then be pursued either to stop the infringing commercial activities, or alternatively to seek a licence revenue.
- A number of Internet sites appeared in the 1990s whereby organizations could advertise technology, and associated intellectual property, to potential licensees. At this time yet2.com is the largest remaining example servicing the needs of industry.

- Reviews can be undertaken of likely business or technology areas to identify potential licensing opportunities. Here the identification, and prioritization, of areas to review is a significant challenge; ultimately, the accurate focusing of these reviews can only be achieved through the effective networking of an organization's legal, commercial and technical personnel.
- Finally, and perhaps most importantly, employees are often aware of licensing opportunities, but for a number of reasons can be reluctant to bring these to the attention of management. Here incentives, and a mixture of formal and information reviews, can be used to highlight such opportunities.

(3) Having identified potential licensees, the following are probably the key criteria to be used in identifying the preferred licensee:

- Does the technology complement, or compete, with the licensee's product ranges – both now and in the future?
- Does the technology produce cost savings for, or take advantage of, the licensee's existing manufacturing, distribution and sales bases?
- What is the strength of the potential licensee's presence in this market, and is this an advantage or a weakness?
- Is the licensee able to fully exploit the market, either directly or through sub-licensing?

In summary, which licensee has the greatest ability and incentive to fully exploit the technology?

There is a vast range of information sources that can be used when seeking to gather the above information. These are traditionally broken down into two types:

- Primary sources – the licensor's employees, consultants, attendance at trade fairs, and so on.
- Secondary sources (that is, published and public sources) - such as patents, annual reports and information gathered by specialist firms involved in competitor intelligence.

NEGOTIATIONS

The licensor can approach potential licensees through a number of routes:

- If there are existing technical contacts, these can be used to initiate contact.
- If the licensor believes its rights are being infringed, there may be merit in using the licensee's legal department as the first point of contact.
- By direct contact with a technology or commercial manager.
- Any material provided should be targeted, and show the benefit of the technology to the potential licensee by addressing many of the questions highlighted in the previous sections.

In most commercial negotiations each side will be seeking a win-lose outcome, that is, one side will seek to maximize its income at the expense of the other party. However, in the case of licence negotiations it is invariably in the licensor's interest to reach a win-win situation.

This position arises because most licences have a running royalty, in which the licensor's income will increase in proportion to the licensee's success in exploiting the licensed intellectual assets. Therefore, it is in the licensor's interest to structure the deal to ensure the commercial success of the licensee. For example, it may be in the licensor's long-term interest to agree a low initial royalty rate, or even a royalty holiday, so the new business is not burdened with high start-up costs.

However, it is generally a far from simple task to assess if the licensee's requests for concessions are in the interest of both parties, or just the licensee's. A licensor will therefore have to be extremely well prepared to reach a satisfactory outcome.

Preparation

In preparing for negotiations with any licensee the following should be considered.

(1) Are there any overarching issues that need to be borne in mind during negotiations, such as:

- Is there a need to establish, or maintain, a long-term working relationship with the licensee?

- Who is more likely to dictate terms in the negotiation – in other words, who has the most attractive alternatives to a signed licence?

(2) What is the licensor's minimum negotiating position, alternatives and priorities:

- Should the focus be on maximizing licence income, gaining rights to improvements, or winning subcontract work, and so on?
- How should royalties be extracted – running royalties, up-front payments, annual payments, payments when milestones are hit, equity transfers (or combinations of these) – and when?
- Does the licensee need to be encouraged to fully exploit the market – should the licensee be given specific performance targets, should the licence have set renewal periods, should the licensee be required to make minimum payments, and so on?
- What market segment should be ceded to this licensee – either directly or by their ability to sub-license? If market restrictions are needed, should these apply to the point of use, manufacture or sale?
- Are there any risks that can be accepted, and are there any that should be passed on?
- What rights to improvements should be sought or given?
- Should product liability, and other warranties, be given by the licensee? Will this need to be supported by insurance cover; if so is a cap on liability acceptable?
- Is the licensee likely to want to perform any acts that should require the licensor's consent?
- Does the licensor need the ability to take action against infringers?
- Does the licensor need to control the prosecution of any patents, and who should pay for any ongoing costs?

(3) What is likely to be the licensee's minimum negotiating position, alternatives and priorities:

- Is the licensee looking for freedom to operate, a monopoly or access to know-how?
- What percentage royalty would make a licence unattractive – what is the licensee's alternative to a licence?
- When will the opportunity enabled by the licence be capable of supporting a licence fee?
- What exit arrangements is the licensee likely to seek?

- Does the licensee need the ability to onward license?
- When could it become attractive for the potential licensee to challenge the patent's validity, rather than enter into a licence?
- Are there economic design-around options for the licensee or its competitors?
- Could any access by the licensor to improvements (if required) undermine the licensee's market position?
- Should the licensee have the ability to take action against infringers?
- Are there any intellectual assets, such as source code or formulation data, that the licensor will be unwilling to release, but which the licensee will need to access if the licensor defaults on the licence, or cease to trade? If so, is an escrow[5] arrangement an option?

(4) When deciding what royalty rate to seek it is wise to use a number of valuation methods to determine a reasonable rate. Several methods are discussed in Chapter 16, but include:

- rules of thumb, that is, 25 per cent of licensee's profit;
- industry, licensee and licensor's average royalty rates;
- calculations based on detailed business models of the licensee's operation.

(5) Finally, all the threads discussed above need to be pulled together before negotiations start, by deciding:

- Whether there is sufficient commonality to reach a sustainable agreement?
- What should be the first offer, and how close should it be to the minimum position?
- What concessions can be ceded during negotiations?

The negotiations themselves

Sound preparation is therefore key to successful licence negotiations. In addition it is important to establish the correct atmosphere for the negotiations themselves. This normally involves the following:

---

5   The licensor places the information in question with an escrow agent; an agreement is then struck between licensor, licensee and escrow agent to define the circumstances under which the information will be released by the escrow agent to the licensee.

- Establishing a friendly and open dialogue – if there are individuals who know, and get on with, members of the other team, consideration should be given to including them in the meetings. It is also useful to start the negotiations on relatively safe and non-confrontational issues.
- Having a clear opening negotiating position.
- Keeping a record of the points that have been agreed and those that remain to be resolved.
- When the negotiations move on to royalties, it is often advisable that any offer, or counter offer, is backed by an explanation of the rationale. Where agreement on royalties proves difficult it may be possible for both sides to agree a valuation approach and negotiate around the data (sales volume, start-up costs, and so on) required by the methodology. If this achieves nothing else, it will normally help both sides understand the business model and key issues they need to agree.

The negotiations will also be aided by operating against an agreed agenda with clear goals. In general the first meeting should concentrate on identifying the important issues and potential sticking points – rather than seeking to resolve them. Key points in an initial agenda might therefore be:

- understanding what intellectual assets the licensee needs to access, and how these will be exploited;
- understanding what intellectual assets the licensors have, and are able to grant access to;
- the disclosure of pertinent background information, especially any issues that are likely to prove to be stumbling blocks during the negotiations;
- A quick run-through of the structure of the licence, with a view to identifying the principal issues that will need detailed negotiation.

CHAPTER 15

AGREEMENTS

LICENCES

For ease of understanding, a licence is normally divided into a number of standard sections. The headings from these sections are used below to highlight the major issues that need to be considered in licence drafting.

Parties

This section should identify the legal entities that will be party to the agreement. It may seem self-evident who the parties are; however, it may make sense to check that:

- the licensor either has ownership of, or the right to onward license, the intellectual property in question (for instance, on occasion, it can transpire that another group company is actually the IP owner and may therefore need to be a party to the licence);
- each party has the power to enter into the agreement – this may involve a check on each party's Memorandum and Articles of Association, as well as the delegated authorities of those signing the licence.

Confusion can often arise if one party has wrongly assumed that all group companies will have rights, by default, under the agreement; however, this is not the case unless specifically prescribed. Rights and obligations will only rest with those legal entities identified as being party to the agreement.

Whereas clauses

Whereas clauses are included to describe the background to, and purpose of, the licence. This can be a useful summary of both parties' intent to enable future readers to gain a quick understanding of the intent of the agreement.

However, this section of the licence is often not essential and care needs to be taken that the text is accurate, and does not prejudice the interests of either party.

Definitions

This will seek to define any frequently used terms in the agreement. Where a word is started in upper case this indicates that it is a defined term, for example, "Licensed Rights" is a defined term, "licensed rights" is not. A range of terms may need to be defined, such as:

- Intellectual property rights will generally need to be defined by reference to a description or a list.
- Where royalty payments are to be made, then terms such as unit price or net invoiced price are likely to need definition.
- Territory will need to be defined if the licensee's rights are being restricted to certain territories.

Grant

This section defines the rights being given to the licensee, and those being retained by the licensor. There are three types of grant:

- Non-exclusive, where the licensor is free to grant further licences to other parties.
- Sole, where the licensor is unable to grant further licences, but can continue to use the intellectual property.
- Exclusive, where the licensor is unable either to grant further licences, or use the intellectual property.

These rights can be limited by market and time. For instance, a licensee could be granted exclusive manufacture rights in the US, and non-exclusive rights elsewhere. Such restrictions can be applied to manufacturing, sale, renting, and so on. However, consideration should be given to how such controls are likely to work in practice. For instance, a licensee may be given the right to manufacture and sell products only in specific geographic regions. Here thought will need to be given to whether such a limitation on sales is enforceable – for instance, what happens if products are bought by a third party and then sold on into a territory that the licensor wanted to exploit either itself, or by providing licence to another manufacturer? In these instances it would be necessary to require the original licensee to ensure that its customers enter into an undertaking not to resell products into such restricted territories.

It is also important to clearly identify what rights are being granted – is the licensee able to make, use, sell, copy, transmit, make derivative works, and so on.

The ability of the licensee to grant sub-licences will also need to be defined. It is common for the licensee's right to sub-licence to be conditional on the consent of the licensor. Here, the agreement often states that this consent cannot be unreasonably withheld, that is, the interests of the licensor would need to be compromised by such a licence for permission to be refused.

The consideration

The licence should describe when royalty payments are due and how they will be determined. There are a number of ways in which royalties can be structured, for example:

- a one-off payment;
- a regular fixed fee, regardless of sales volume;
- a fixed fee per item sold or produced by the licensee;
- a fee dependent on the income received by the licensee;
- trigger events can be used to specify when royalties should start, stop or be changed;
- and so on including combinations of the above.

There are a number of issues that need to be considered when defining the way royalties will be determined:

- The licensor will wish to ensure the royalty regime incentivizes the licensee to fully exploit the market and hence generate the maximum royalty for the licensor. This is especially important where an exclusive licence is being provided – a licensor will not wish to find it has granted an exclusive licence, under which its income is related only to a licensee's sales, to an organization that it eventually transpires is only interested in preventing the technology entering the market place.

- Where royalties are attached to the sale of products or services it is important that these terms are accurately defined. For example, it is important that licensees cannot reduce their royalty payments by splitting the product or service into sub-components, and potentially only paying royalties on the sale from a low value sub-component.

- Care needs to be taken that royalty payments are triggered by all the routes open to the licensee to generate revenue from the licensed intellectual property, that is, use, hire, sale, onward licensing, use as collateral, manufacture, and so on.

- Where rights are being provided to a mixture of both know-how and patents, and the agreement could continue past the expiry of the patents, then to avoid the agreement becoming legally invalid in certain countries it may be necessary to identify what proportion of the royalty is related to the know-how and which to patents, so that royalties can be adjusted once the patents have expired.

- It may also be appropriate to consider whether the licensor should gain a return if the licensee, or that part of the licensee's business exploiting the licensed intellectual property, is sold. This is especially important if intellectual property is licensed into a start-up company, where the largest income stream could be that received from the sale of the business, rather than initial product runs. In this case it may be appropriate for the licensor to receive a proportion of the sale/flotation price of the business.

The licensor sometimes grants a licensee "most favoured terms" here an undertaking is given not to license the intellectual property to another organization on more favourable terms than that provided to such a licensee.

The term

The life, or term, of the agreement will need to be defined – either as a fixed period, or in relation to the life of the intellectual property. It may also be appropriate to define the right of each party to extend the term of the agreement.

Accountancy provisions

These clauses will define the records the licensee must keep and submit, to enable the licensor to determine the royalty payments. The licensor may also insist on the right to audit the licensee to ensure these records are accurate. This section of the licence will also need to:

- identify the bank account into which the royalties should be deposited;
- define the currency in which payments should be made;
- state when payments should be made;
- describe the penalties for late payment.

Improvements

Each party's rights to improvements made by either the licensor or licensee should be defined. The licence will thus need to:

- define improvement (for example this could be any intellectual property that infringes the licensed IPRs; any intellectual property that might reasonably be of commercial interest in the exploitation of the licensed intellectual property; intellectual property that provides features that can be incorporated in the licensed products/services, and so on);
- describe each party's obligations to notify the other of any improvements they may make;
- describe who should own such improvements, who has the right to decide how they will be protected and how the costs from such activities will be met;
- define each party's respective rights to these improvements.

Note: A grant forward provision defines the licensee's rights to improvement made by the licensor. A grant back provision defines the licensor's rights to improvements made by the licensee.

Confidentiality

There are likely to be restrictions on both parties' ability to release and use generated and received confidential information. If the licence does include such restrictions it will be necessary to define what constitutes commercial information. If it is not possible to explicitly list such information then it will be necessary to develop a description. Such a description may be anchored in its general characteristics that are:

- It is not generally known in the trade or business.
- Its economic value is, in part, a result of its limited availability.
- It is the subject of efforts to maintain its secrecy.

Depending on the importance, and sensitivity, of the information it may also be appropriate to define the standard of care to be followed in its use and management: it is relatively common to state that the licensee shall treat the licensor's information to the same standard as its own. However, this may sometimes be insufficiently rigorous. Alternatively, examples can be given of the minimum acceptable standard of care, that is: information will be kept in a locked cabinet when not in use; where information is kept on a computer network, access shall be limited to identified individuals with a need to know, and so on. It is also possible to list the situations where the information can be used, such as for setting process parameters in a given plant, on a need-to -know basis only, and so on.

Licensor's obligations

Here provisions may be needed, for example, to define:

- the obligations placed on the licensor to keep intellectual property rights in force;
- what assistance and information the licensor will provide – here it may be appropriate to describe both minimum and maximum levels of support.

Licensee's obligations

The licensee's obligations should be identified. These could include the following:

- To fully exploit the market. There may simply be a statement that the licensor will use all reasonable endeavours to fully exploit the market; alternatively there may be a more detailed list of targets that must be met, or actions to be undertaken.
- It is usual to define the way in which the licensor's name will, or will not be used, by the licensee. This could, for instance, require the licensee to make reference to the licensor in marketing material and/or labelling on packaging. Conversely, there may be a bar on the use of the licensor's name.
- A requirement on the licensee to manufacture any articles to an agreed specification.

Warranties and indemnities

Note: A warranty is where one party gives specified assurances to another; while an indemnity is an undertaking to make compensation available if certain events do, or do not, take place.

The following undertakings are typically provided in this section:

- The licensor may warrant that it owns the intellectual property being licensed; or alternatively has the right to enter into the licence.
- The licensor may warrant that it is unaware of any third party rights that would be infringed by the licensee's use of the intellectual property.
- The licensee may be required to indemnify the licensor against all costs, claims, damages and expenses that could arise out of the licensee's use of the intellectual property. As part of this provision the licensee may be required to take out appropriate insurance cover; the licensor is most likely to insist on such protection when the licensee's financial reserves are limited.
- There may also be provisions to limit one or more of the party's liabilities; this can take the form of a defined cap, or alternatively the limit of liability may be set at the aggregate value of the income stream received under the licence.

There are occasions when the licensee will ask for an undertaking that the exploitation of the licensed intellectual property will not infringe third party rights. This request normally arises in one of two situations:

- Where the licensee is unfamiliar with the legal aspects of intellectual property, and believes this is a reasonable request (it is generally not as this type of warranty is testifying to the rights held by third parties, rather than the rights held by the licensor).
- Where the licensee is in a very strong negotiating position, as can arise when the licence is part of a larger commercial arrangement, and the licensor has little choice but to concede.

Infringement

The licence should clearly state what will happen in the event that a third party is found to be infringing the licensed intellectual property. Specifically, this will need to define who is able to take action against infringers, who bears the cost of taking action and who receives any damages.

Where the licence is exclusive then the licensee will often be given the right to take action. However, where there is a non-exclusive grant then it may be more difficult to decide who should take action.

Even when the licensee is given the right to take action against infringers the licensor may feel that it is appropriate for it to receive a proportion of any settlement reached as it is its intellectual property that has generated the compensation.

The agreement may also contain a provision allowing royalty payments to be reduced, or suspended, under certain circumstances, for example while third party infringement is taking place, in the event that no action is taken against an alleged infringer, or if any action taken against the infringer is lost.

Arbitration

The licence may specify the arrangements to be followed in the case of a dispute that the parties are unable to resolve amongst themselves. This will normally provide for mediation or arbitration:

- *Mediation*: The mediator will be trained, and accredited, in dispute resolution. A mediator's role is to help the parties resolve any dispute; they cannot impose a settlement.
- *Arbitration*: Arbitration is generally binding on both parties, and is therefore similar in concept to litigation. However, arbitration will generally be quicker and cheaper.

Termination

This should identify who, if anyone, is able to terminate the licence and under what circumstances. The situations described could include:

- failure to pay royalty payments;
- breach of confidentiality obligations;
- whether either the licensee or licensor have the right to unilaterally terminate the licence.

This clause should also describe what rights and activities survive the termination, that is, which activities are allowed to be wound down, which must stop on termination and which can continue after the expiry of the licence.

The format of the licence arrangement

The licence will need to be either "under seal" or "under hand". For a licence that has no consideration to be legally binding it must be under seal, in which case it must be counter signed by one or more witnesses.

Boilerplate clauses

This section is used to group the remaining background clauses that do not fit under the above headings. These may include:

- the contact points for correspondence;
- which country's laws will be used to interpret the licence;
- whether any of the rights and obligations can be assigned.

UNIVERSITY RESEARCH AGREEMENTS

There are a number of reasons why public and private organizations may choose to sponsor research at Universities. These include:

- It can provide access to skills and expertise not available through other routes.
- University tariffs tend, in general, to be lower than in industry.
- The sponsor's financial input to the project can be leveraged by access to grants.
- The sponsorship can help build relationships that can be useful in lobbying government, local authorities, pressure groups, and so on.

However, the use of universities does come with a number of disadvantages:

- Individual researchers and departments are judged on the quality, and number, of publications. Therefore, there is pressure on researchers to publish the result of their work, which will often not be in the interests of the sponsor.
- It can be difficult to achieve the transfer of knowledge from the university to the sponsor.
- A lot of time and effort can be spent negotiating contracts, especially the intellectual property clauses.

- The timing and progress of research is often dictated by the use of students who have a fixed period to complete the work and write up their theses.

As a result many organizations will only place long-term research with Universities and restrict such contracts to technology areas they regard as enabling.

Intellectual property provisions within university agreements

The research agreement must:

- describe the rights, and obligations, each part has in respect of background and arising intellectual property;
- confirm who will own arising intellectual property;
- describe the basis of compensation for the university and creators/ inventors if the intellectual property is used or commercially exploited.

These are considered below.

Rights to background intellectual property

Universities are often unwilling to grant rights to their background intellectual property within a research agreement; instead they will often seek to postpone negotiations until such time as exploitation is due to take place. This will often be unacceptable to the sponsor who will not wish to start negotiating a licence, for what is likely to be a poorly defined pool of intellectual property, after the research is complete. Instead the sponsor will want the research agreement to clearly identify any ongoing costs and commitments.

There can also be disagreement about the value of any background intellectual property. In general, unless there are background patents or valuable data, the sponsor will be unwilling to make significant payments to background IP. If the background intellectual property is simply know-how, the sponsor will argue that he or she is already paying for access within the tariffs described in the research agreement.

Figure 15.1 can be used to help characterize whether a low (probably zero) royalty is appropriate or whether the university does have grounds for requesting a royalty for access to background intellectual property.

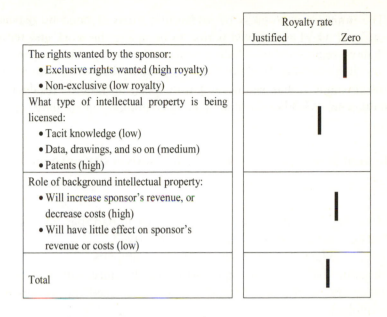

	Royalty rate	
	Justified	Zero
The rights wanted by the sponsor: • Exclusive rights wanted (high royalty) • Non-exclusive (low royalty)		I
What type of intellectual property is being licensed: • Tacit knowledge (low) • Data, drawings, and so on (medium) • Patents (high)	I	
Role of background intellectual property: • Will increase sponsor's revenue, or decrease costs (high) • Will have little effect on sponsor's revenue or costs (low)		I
Total		I

Figure 15.1   Valuation of background IP

Ownership, and rights to, arising intellectual property
This is often the most difficult area to resolve within the negotiations. The university will often wish to own the arising intellectual property on the premise that it needs ownership to ensure its ability to generate a revue through the use of the intellectual property outside of the sponsor's area of interest. However, the intellectual property is typically the contract's main deliverable, and the sponsor will generally argue that it should own what it has effectively purchased. Ultimately, this is really an argument over principles; neither party needs to own the intellectual property to gain the exploitation rights and controls it needs; instead these can be defined within a licence from the owner. In reality the key issues to debate are:

- Who has rights to each market?
- What royalties should be paid to the other party?
- Who pays the prosecution of any patents and manages the prosecution process?

Recently, there has been a tendency for certain universities to initially refuse to grant the sponsor default rights to any intellectual property; but instead to offer a time limited option, during which the sponsor is given the right to enter in negotiations to take a licence to arising and background intellectual property. Unless the university is in an extremely strong negotiating position this is unlikely to be acceptable to any sponsor. This tactic is systematic of a much more aggressive negotiating stance taken by universities in recent years. Inevitably this has resulted in the negotiations becoming more difficult and time consuming, and as a consequence many sponsors have decided to reduce the level of R&D they place with universities.

CHAPTER 16

VALUATION OF INTELLECTUAL ASSETS

The valuation of intellectual assets is an area receiving increased attention, with many organizations seeking to develop tools able to value intellectual property and other intellectual assets. This drive is in response to a number of pressures, including:

- a need to monitor trends in the value of such assets, thereby identifying problems, and further assessing whether management initiatives are succeeding in improving their value;
- a need to understand the difference in the value ascribed to an organization as a whole, as often evidenced in their stock market value, and the value of their fixed assets;
- a need for data to assist in the licensing, acquisition or disposal of assets either to group companies or third parties.

However, as is witnessed by the increasing use of key performance indicators (KPIs) and metrics it is not always necessary, or desirable, for management to resort to the use of financial measures. For example, if the value of a project is known, then the utility of a patent will often be adequately represented by a simple metric showing whether the relevant project's commercial success is dependent on that patent. Nevertheless, care must be taken when using metrics as both the reviewer and the audience must have a common understanding of what aspect of the asset is being measured, and how this attribute is represented. A system of metrics should therefore only be developed once there is a clear understanding of how it will be used. External stakeholders, the Board and line managers will all have very different demands.

A financial value does not have these problems as it is generally simpler to interpret. However, the valuation of intellectual assets is not an exact science and is rarely simple.

This chapter looks at a number of approaches that can be used to value intellectual assets, as well as the types of metrics organizations may wish to use as alternatives.

FINANCIAL VALUATION

There are many methods that can be used to value intellectual assets, although these are all derived from three basic approaches.

Income	
This approach seeks to calculate directly the improvement in profit margin likely to result from the use of a given intellectual asset.	Examples: ■ A reduction in the resources required to complete a task due to the availability of performance data. ■ The availability of design specifications that enable an organization to outsource manufacturing work using competitive tendering. ■ An increase in profit margin resulting from a competitor's inability to enter a market as a result of patent coverage.

Market	
This approach seeks to determine the value of an intellectual asset by reference to another asset having a known value.	Examples: ■ There may be a licence between two unrelated parties where similar intellectual property or assets were valued. ■ Similar articles which have been traded independently.

Cost	
This approach seeks to measure the cost of either replacing or reproducing the intellectual asset.	Examples: ▪ Cost of creating an engineering design. ▪ The cost of the research and development required to develop a technology.

Each method has its strengths and weaknesses. The following table seeks to indicate which are best suited to various intellectual assets[1]:

Method	Primary	Secondary	Weak
Patents and technology	Income	Market	Cost
Trademarks and brands	Income	Market	Cost
Copyrights	Income	Market	Cost
Distribution networks	Cost	Income	Market
Corporate practices and procedures	Cost	Income	Market
Product software	Income	Market	Cost

The following examples show how each of these approaches work in practice.

Income approaches

The Income approach considers the cumulative improvement in margins likely to result from the use of the intellectual asset. These improved margins can arise in the following areas:

- *Premium pricing*: Here the method is concerned with the additional revenue the business receives through the use of the asset.
- *Cost savings*: Here the method is concerned with the cost savings afforded by access to the intellectual assets.
- *Excess operating profits*: Here the method is concerned with the increase in profit that is afforded by the combined effect of cost savings and premium pricing.

---

1   G.V. Smith and Russell L. Parr, *Valuation of Intellectual Property and Intangible Assets*, John Wiley, New York, 1994.

The Income method takes into account all cash flows and uncertainties. However, it requires a detailed knowledge of the market and business.

This approach can be demonstrated using a simple example, in which an "idea" is tracked through its various development stages from initial investigation to production.

	Initial investigation	Prototype production	Production set up	Market launch	Production

The following table presents the cost, income and probability data needed to undertake this analysis.

Probability of failure at each stage	50%	10%	10%	5%	0%
Expenditure/ income from activity	–£10 k	–£100 k	–£500 k	–£100 k	£1 m/a turnover, 30% profit for 10 years

The product's development is shown below as a decision tree – there are clearly five possible outcomes of which four are failure modes.

We now need to calculate the financial impact, and probability, of each outcome.

Cumulative probability of outcome	50%	5%	4.5%	2%	38.5%
Cumulative expenditure/ income	–£10 k	–£110 k	–£610 k	–£710 k	£2290 k
Value	–£5 k	–£5.5 k	–£27.5 k	–£14.5 k	£881.7 k

By summing the values of each outcome we end up with a total value for the project of £829.2 k.

The impact of a given intellectual asset can then be mapped on to this decision tree. For example, the impact of existing know-how used in designing a production line for the new product can be introduced into the assessment, both in terms of the savings resulting from not having to develop this know-how and, presumably, a reduction in the likelihood of failure. This will generate a different value for the project – the difference clearly being the value of this know-how to the project.

However, the approach as described so far has a weakness – we have assumed that £1 received today is worth the same as £1 received in several years' time – this is not the case. The Income method therefore normally uses a discount rate, called the "cost of capital", to mark-down the value of future income and expenditure, and translate these figures into a net present value (NPV).

Using a cost of capital figure of 8 per cent per annum (a typical rate used by accountants) and assuming each development stage takes one year, we can now tabulate the expenditure incurred during a successful product launch:

The present day value (that is, discounted value) is determined by multiplying the cumulative discount rate by the cash flow

The value is the sum of the discounted cash flow and the probability of the income appearing

Year	Cash flow	Discount rate	Disc'ed cash	Prob of event	Prob * NPV
Now	−10	1	−10	1.0	−10
+1	−100	0.92	−92	0.5	−46
+2	−500	0.846	−423.2	0.45	−190.44
+3	−100	0.779	−77.87	0.405	−31.54
+4	300	0.716	214.92	0.365	82.74
+5	300	0.659	197.72	0.365	76.12
+6	300	0.606	181.91	0.365	70.03
+7	300	0.558	167.35	0.365	64.43
+8	300	0.513	153.97	0.365	59.28
+9	300	0.472	141.65	0.365	54.53
+10	300	0.434	130.32	0.365	50.17
+11	300	0.4	119.89	0.365	46.16
+12	300	0.368	110.30	0.365	42.47
+13	300	0.338	101.48	0.365	39.07
				Total	307.03k

The value of the income stream, in the event the project is successful, is therefore £307.03 k. However, we now need to do a similar analysis for the four other possible outcomes (that is, the possible futures in which money was spent, but the project failed). Summing across all outcomes we end up with a value of £265.2 k. This value is termed the project's net present value.

The above example is relatively simple; in a more realistic and complex business scenario these analyses can become computationally complicated and are generally handled by spreadsheets.

It is worth noting that in the previous analysis we failed to attribute a value to the original "idea". In many instances, especially licence negotiations, it is important to have a method of valuing this original idea.

A value can be deduced as follows:

Most industries and organizations have an agreed rate of return they typically expect to make from an investment. This is called the industry rate of return or internal rate of return (IRR). The analysis presented here can be rerun to determine the value of the "idea" that is consistent with the project achieving this IRR.

This calculation is performed by simply replacing the cost of capital figure (8 per cent) with the relevant IRR figure (a typical figure is 12 per cent). The value of the project so calculated can be ascribed to the value of the "idea"; in this instance its value is £118.6 k.

It should be noted that with this analysis it is possible to end up with a negative value for the "idea". However, this will only occur when the project is forecast to generate less profit than the organization would normally expect to make from the investment/risks it is being asked to take, and hence the project should probably not proceed.

Note: In a licence negotiation it is quite likely that the licensee will be unwilling to share the type of information needed to perform the above assessment. As a result this approach may not be suitable for settling debate between licensee and licensor on the value of licensed intellectual assets. However, it will enable the licensee to get a clear picture of the true value of the idea.

Market approaches

The determination of an intellectual asset's value requires the identification of a comparable transaction, that is, its value is determined by reference to the known value of similar intellectual assets.

When valuing intellectual assets, the search for a comparable market transaction can become almost futile. This is not because finding a comparable transaction amongst a long list of sales and licences data is difficult, but because intellectual assets are generally not developed to be sold and hence data is very scarce.

However, at the simplest level there are a number of well-established rules-of-thumb that, while only capable of providing rough guidance, have been successfully used for many years:

- *The 25 per cent rule*: it is often assumed that as a default 25 per cent of the profit made from an enterprise can be fairly attributed to its intellectual assets.
- *The relative value of patents and know-how*: a number of court cases have ruled that, as a default, it is appropriate to attribute 25 to 33 per cent of the value of a bundle of intellectual assets to the patents.

Cost approaches

This approach seeks to measure the cost of either replacing or reproducing the intellectual asset:

- The cost of reproduction is based on the cost of independently reproducing the asset from the initial concept to its current configuration.
- The cost of replacement seeks to establish the cost of replacing the asset with the nearest available alternative.

Examples include:

- Cost of creating an engineering design.
- The sunk cost of research and development required to develop a given technology.

Such a valuation should take into account:

- overheads
- salaries and related costs
- external costs
- capital investment, and so on.

Once a replacement or reproduction cost has been determined then adjustments will be made to take into account depreciation or obsolescence.

The advantage of this approach is that it is generally quick. However, it is unsuitable for the valuation of most intellectual assets, for a number of reasons, including:

- It is not based on the economic benefit derived from the asset.
- The impact and strength of competitors' position are not taken into account.
- Risks and uncertainties are ignored.

These limitations are demonstrated if we try and apply this approach to the example examined previously. Specifically, the value of the "idea" simply becomes the cost involved in its creation. Depending on the circumstances this could range from the cost of an inventor sitting and thinking for five minutes, to the cost of a major R&D department working round the clock for five years.

The Market and Income approaches both place a value on the "idea" in the range £100 k to £150 k. If we assume that the internal costs of a single researcher is c.£75 k/a, and further assume that the researcher comes up with one "idea" of this type every two years, then the Cost approach generates a similar number. However, equally likely scenarios will yield very different values.

The relief from royalty approach

The "relief from royalty" technique seeks to determine what royalty an organization would expect to pay a third party if they owned the intellectual assets in question. The technique is a variation of the Income approach, but in this case a value is determined by multiplying a royalty rate by the income or profit stream. This is the most frequently used method in transfer price determinations and many other instances.

Any valuation exercise using a relief from royalty approach still needs access to a large number of transactions to identify a comparable royalty rate. Fortunately, information can be sourced from a range of external publications and Internet sites. In addition, the large accountancy firms have built up bodies of data which can be used, for a price, in these analyses. The following are typical of the data sets such sources[2] can provide:

	Median royalty rates	*Average operating profits*	*Royalty as % of profit*
Electronics	4.5%	8.8%	51.2%
Semiconductors	2.5%	29.3%	8.5%
Telecom	5.0%	15.9%	26.7%

However, even with access to data covering a large number of transactions it will rarely be possible to identify an identical comparable transaction. Inevitably, a valuation exercise will start with a similar transaction or a range of industry norms – adjustments will then need to be made to take account of differences between the comparable transaction and the asset being valued.

If we seek to use this approach to value the "idea" discussed previously then the analysis looks as follows.

As previously highlighted we need to start with a comparable transaction, or make reference to an industry-average royalty rate. Let us assume that, in this market, licensed intellectual assets are typically valued at between 2 per cent and 6 per cent of turnover.

	Low	*Medium*	*High*
Royalty rate	2%	4%	6%

The analysis now examines a range of criteria to establish if our example should be at the top or bottom of this range. Typical criteria considered in this type of analysis are given below, together with hypothetical scores. It should be noted that even in a real analysis these scores tend not to be produced using a rigorous methodology, but instead by establishing the consensus of a workshop involving technical, commercial and IP personnel.

---

2   R. Goldscheider, J. Jarosz and C. Mulhern, 'Use of the 25 Percent Rule in Valuing IP', *Les Nouvelles*, Dec 2002.

	Low	Medium	High
Profit margin				
Turnover				
Life of product/ service				
Level of investment				
Certainty of competitive position				
Certainty of technical position				
Overall score				

In this case the analysis produces a royalty rate a little below the average of 3 per cent of turnover. Applying this royalty rate to the example used previously, in which the turnover was £1 m/a, yields a value of £30 k/a. Discounting this income by using 8 per cent as the cost of capital, we end up with £151.9 k as the idea's value.

As with the pure income approach, the relief from royalty approach can be used to look at the value of an intellectual asset generating value via premium pricing, cost savings or excess operating profits.

Valuation of immature intellectual assets

There are circumstances where intellectual assets ideally need to be valued before their utility and application are clear – this situation is encountered most frequently during licence negotiations between universities and industry.

When immature intellectual assets are being licensed the licensor may suggest that the licence simply states that royalties will be agreed at some point in the future when their value can be more readily calculated. However, delaying negotiations is rarely in the interests of the licensee, who will fear having to start negotiations at a time when the technology is proven, and perhaps after they have already invested significant time and money in its development. Clearly under these circumstances the licensor will be in a very strong negotiating position, while the licensee's will have been undermined. Therefore the licensee will generally wish to reach agreement on the royalty rate, or at least a valuation method, before it has made any investment.

Recently, universities have been offering options to licence intellectual assets, where industry reserves the right, for a fixed time period, to enter into negotiations. However, this is rarely attractive to industry unless the agreement proposes a value or valuation method, as again their negotiating position will be weakened with time.

METRICS

The alignment of an organization's intellectual asset portfolio to business strategy should be regularly reviewed and reported. This can be assisted by the use of metrics focusing on:

- The intellectual asset's "role". Here metrics will seek to measure the potential importance of a given asset-type to business success. For example, in a market where there are a large number of interchangeable or cheap-to-develop technologies, then the role of patents will generally be limited. However, in a market where there are a limited number of expensive-to-develop technical solutions then the role of patents can be much more significant.
- The "utility" of the intellectual asset. Here metrics will seek to measure whether a given asset is fit for purpose. For example, in a business where patents have a significant role then a patent with broad, granted, claims may have a high utility. However, where patents have a limited role then their utility will similarly be restricted.

Hence a service, project or product which has a high role for patents should ideally have a high utility patent portfolio. Conversely, if there is a limited role for patents then the expense in maintaining a high utility portfolio may be not justified. Any mismatch between metrics therefore indicates a problem.

There are four basic ways in which intellectual assets can impact on a product, service or project's profitability. Each of these needs to be considered when developing the system of metrics:

- Reducing costs – for example, manufacturing, distribution, marketing, and so on.
- Increasing sales – either in terms of sales volume or the speed of market penetration.

- Enabling a price premium to be charged either through actual or perceived product/service differentiation.
- Increasing competitors' costs by limiting their manufacturing, distribution or marketing options.

The following are a few examples of the issues that should be considered when developing metrics designed to determine the role and utility of a patent or trademark.

Patents

Issues to consider when determining the role of patents:

- The commercial importance of the technology protected by the patents.
- In practice are patents capable of restricting commercially damaging competitor, customer, supplier or distributor activity?
- Are patents the best method of restricting competitor, customer, supplier or distributor's activities?

Issues to consider when determining the utility of existing patent:

- Once granted will the patent(s) provide a real barrier?
- What is the probability of a strong patent(s) being won?
- Can the patent(s) be enforced?

As in the case of the market approach to valuation, an overall score for each metric can be determined in a workshop typically involving commercial, technical and R&D personnel.

Brands

Issues to consider when determining the role of branding:

- Does branding have an effect on price in this market sector (or is the product purchased on the basis of technical differentiation, and so on)?
- Does branding have an effect on sales volume, or the bid success rate, in this market sector (or is the volume determined by price, relationships with the distributors, and so on)?
- How durable are brands (how expensive and what time is required for a competitor to establish a brand)?

- How significant are the sales of related products under the same brand?

Issues to consider when determining the utility of an existing brand:

- What levels of mark-up are being achieved compared to industry averages and to what extent is this margin due to branding?
- What sales volume is being achieved compared to industry averages and to what extent are these sales due to branding?
- How strong is customer loyalty compared to industry standard (level of repeat business) and to what extent are these sales due to branding?
- Is the brand sufficiently well established to prevent copying or has a trademark been registered?
- Are there changes likely in the market that could undermine the brand?

If appropriate this type of assessment can be performed for all the intellectual assets supporting a product, service or organization. This data can then be presented in a simple table as shown below.

It is not always necessary to produce detailed scores – often a simple high/medium/low gradation is sufficient.

Asset	Need	Utility	Diff/Enabler
Patent	High	High	
Trademark	Low	Low	
Manufacturing know-how	Medium	Low	Differentiator
Relationship with distribution network	High	Low	Enabler

It is also often worth highlighting "enablers" and "differentiators"

Most organizations will already have a well-established system of key performance indicators (KPIs) to which these intellectual asset metrics can be added if appropriate.

VALUATION – A FINAL OBSERVATION

The use of metrics, or the valuation of assets, using a rigorous, standardized, methodology will invariably lead to an improved understanding of the business itself including its key strengths, weaknesses, opportunities and threats. Those involved in these exercises will often find that this improved understanding is a significant extra (or even the principal) benefit from any valuation exercises.

CHAPTER 17

DUE DILIGENCE

In the context of intellectual property, due diligence is a term that can be used for two quite different activities. Specifically:

- A review conducted to identify risks, and confirm the value, of a planned merger, acquisition or investment.
- A check performed to ensure the absence of third party intellectual property rights that could prevent an organization from exploiting, selling, or offering to sell, a particular product or service. This is often called a "freedom for use review".

DUE DILIGENCE IN MERGERS, ACQUISITIONS AND INVESTMENTS

Here a due diligence should focus principally on those assets and events that could give rise to risk, or impact on the value of the planned transaction.

Before starting any due diligence it is therefore necessary to gain a clear understanding of the target businesses and the purpose of the transaction, so that the due diligence can be correctly focused. Without this focus a due diligence is liable to degenerate into an audit, in which an attempt is made to catalogue the target's entire intellectual property portfolio, with view to checking that all these assets are in force and can be transferred.

When a business is being split, the purchaser will not only need to secure those intellectual assets necessary to operate the acquired business, but also ensure that the seller does not retain any rights that could restrict the business's future commercial freedoms. Similarly, the seller will wish to ensure that it retains those intellectual assets necessary to operate its remaining businesses, and that it does not cede rights that could be used to restrict its future commercial activities. Such an assessment can only be carried out against a clear understanding of the markets and technologies the seller is ceding, and those where the buyer and seller intend to compete. Unfortunately, in many situations this clarity does not exist.

Depending on the characteristics of the target's business there may be up to four focused activities that should be undertaken, as shown in Figure 17.1.

Unfortunately, the start of a due diligence is traditionally heralded by the acquirer, or their legal advisors, issuing the acquiree with a document requesting a mass of information, which can in extreme cases include copies of all intellectual property agreements and registered intellectual property. Indeed many organizations routinely carrying out due diligence have produced standardized questionnaires used to elicit the maximum (note: quantity rather than quality) amount of information. Once a due diligence starts down this route it is rarely possible to extract any real value from the exercise. The scarce resources that are available will be drawn into gathering, cataloguing and analysing this information.

Another problem frequently encountered is that intellectual property due diligence is often treated as an ancillary exercise compared with the mainstream corporate due diligence. Instead reliance is often placed on ensuring appropriate intellectual property warranties are granted by the seller. However, warranties should not be regarded as an alternative to carrying out an adequate due diligence, as they generally offer poor compensation and are rarely comprehensive.

If there is business-critical intellectual property involved in a transaction, then, once it has been identified, the following tasks can be carried out.

Patents

Where there are important patents, checks can be made:

- that renewal fees have been paid;
- that the registration is in the correct name;
- that there are no third party rights that would hinder their enforcement or use, such as those arising from joint ownership, licences, government funding (which often results in the State reserving certain rights), and so on.

Business characteristics	Focus of the due diligence
How important could any single item of intellectual property be in achieving future business aspirations? Specifically:	
• Does the target currently, and will it continue to, produce a large range of loosely related products or services? If so then a problem with any single item of intellectual property is unlikely to carry a significant business risk, or impact on the value of the transaction.	→ The way intellectual property has been managed should be examined to ensure that poor management practices could not have resulted in endemic intellectual property problems across the range of products or services.
• However, if the target has a limited number of business-critical products or services, then the quality of the underpinning intellectual property could impact on both risk and value.	→ Key intellectual property should be identified and a check made into its validity, life, strength and transferability.
Are there clear boundaries around the transaction? If a business is being split with intellectual property currently owned by a single entity being divided, then time and money will need to be invested in identifying and allocating intellectual property. Further, mechanisms will need to be agreed for resolving any future disputes regarding wrongly allocated intellectual property.	→ A way of defining the intellectual property involved with the transaction will need to be developed – if generic descriptions cannot be developed then individual items of intellectual property will need to be listed. In either case, key intellectual assets should probably be identified, listed and transferability established.
Is the transaction intended to create a limited number of new, high value, market opportunities?	→ The strength of the combined acquiree's and acquirer's intellectual property portfolio may need to be reviewed and the validity, life, and transferability of key acquired intellectual property established.

Figure 17.1   Providing a focus for due diligence reviews

- that no undertakings have been given that would prevent their assignment or sale, either as part of this, or any possible future, transaction;
- that the inventors have assigned their rights to the apparent patent owner;
- that the remaining life of the patents matches business aspirations;
- that the patent scope, and filing programme, provides the required protection;
- that the patents are not being infringed, especially by competitors;
- whether the acquirer will need to grant licensed rights to the seller.

It may also be necessary to check for third party patents that could be infringed by existing, or planned, activities.

Trademarks

Where there are important trademarks, checks can be made:

- that renewal fees have been paid;
- that the registration is in the correct name;
- that there are no third party rights that would hinder their enforcement or use;
- that no undertakings have been given that would prevent their assignment or sale, either as part of this, or any possible future, transaction;
- that there are no grounds on which the trademark could be revoked, such as lack of use, or the name becoming a generic description;
- that the trademark is registered in relevant classes and territories;
- that the trademark is not being infringed;
- whether the acquirer will need to grant licensed rights to the seller.

Copyright

Where there are important copyrighted works, checks can be made:

- that there are no third party rights that would hinder the enforcement of the IPRs or their use;
- that no undertakings have been given that would prevent their assignment or sale, either as part of this, or any possible future, transaction;
- that the authors have assigned their rights to the apparent owner;
- that the copyright is not being infringed by competitors;

- that the life of the protection is appropriate (as this is generally the life of the author plus 70 years, this is unlikely to be a problem with most businesses);
- whether the acquirer needs to retain copies, and if so how will used and third party access be controlled.

Licences

Where the target will continue to need access to intellectual assets licensed in from third parties, then checks need to be made:

- that the grant, royalty provisions, performance targets, termination provisions and term all match the acquiree's business plans;
- that the licence is still in force and that the licensee is not in default;
- that the licence can be assigned, or if the licence is to be retained by the seller that the rights can be onward licensed;
- to establish if the acquiree and seller both need licensed rights, and if so whether this is allowable under the licence.

Where the target's intellectual assets will continue to be licensed to a third party, then checks need to be made:

- that the grant, royalty schedules, performance targets, termination provisions and term will not allow the licensee to compete with the transferred business;
- if the royalties being generated are significant, then assurance should be sought that the licence is still in force and that neither the licensee nor licensor are in default;
- that the licence can be assigned if this is appropriate;
- that any ability to sub-license will not damage new business aspirations.

Confidential information

Organizations rarely have a register of confidential information so it is especially difficult to identify business-critical information or know-how.

However, where confidential information is of value the following checks can be made:

- Do current, or past, employees or contractors have knowledge that could impact on the business if disclosed? If so, are they bound by confidentiality undertakings, and are such undertakings likely to be respected?
- If such confidentiality undertakings were broken would this significantly impact on the benefits of the transaction? If so is this risk too great for the transaction to proceed?
- Are key employees likely to remain in post after the transaction? If not what action is appropriate to retain their services or ensure their silence?

DUE DILIGENCE – FREEDOM FOR USE

If an organization commercially exploits, sells or offers to sell a product or service in violation of a third party's valid intellectual property rights, then it has committed an act of infringement. The holder of the intellectual property right, whether this right is obtained via a licence or by virtue of ownership, can stop any such infringing activity. Alternatively, the holder may seek a royalty in exchange for allowing such commercial activity to continue.

As with other aspects of the law, ignorance is no excuse; if infringement is deemed to have taken place, damages may be awarded by the courts regardless of whether the infringer was aware of the third party rights in question.

It is up to the intellectual property's owner to monitor for infringement of its rights; the State provides no assistance. However, once infringement is identified then the owner is able to make use of national, and international, legal processes to enforce its rights. If legal action is taken and judgement goes against the infringer the courts may award damages. In this instance the damages will be calculated from the date when infringement started, not the date the infringer was made aware of any third party's rights. However, the legal process is fraught with uncertainties; regardless of the merits of the case neither the defendant nor the plaintive will be certain what a judge or jury will decide. For this reason, and the desire to save legal costs, most cases are settled outside of the court system.

There are three main areas that need to be addressed when seeking to avoid the infringement of third party's intellectual property rights:

- Avoiding the unauthorized copying, or distribution, of third party's copyrighted material.
- Ensuring your technologies and capabilities do not become mixed, or contaminated, with that sourced from other organizations unless you have secured clear rights, ideally in perpetuity, to this introduced intellectual property. If rights have not been secured, and this contamination is allowed to take place, it may not be possible to commercialize your own technology without the permission of third parties.
- Ensuring that other organizations do not have intellectual property rights such as patents, trademarks and registered designs and so on that can hinder your commercial activities.

Many organizations may choose to proactively search for third party's intellectual property rights to avoid possible infringement. The focus of such reviews will vary from industry to industry; in the case of the music or film industry then it will involve a check that copyright has been secured to music scores, books and scripts. For manufacturers, checks will often centre on the avoidance of third party patents. In the case of patents are two types of activity that may be undertaken:

- patent monitoring
- due diligence.

Patent monitoring

With patent monitoring regular searches are made for third party patents, published since the last search, using search parameters chosen to match an organization's technical and commercial activities. Patents found are then checked to determine if they would restrict the organization's current and planned activities. When patent monitoring has been carried out over a number of years it will give a reasonable level of confidence that there are no third party patents preventing exploitation of key technologies. However, this approach is not as rigorous as a due diligence (freedom for use review) which is carried out at a key stage in a project's evolution.

Freedom for use review

In the case of an industrial process, or product, a freedom for use review will often focus on:

- reviewing third party patents;

- ensuring no third party intellectual property has been imported without permission.

An organization will need to decide the circumstance under which a freedom for use review will be triggered. For instance, an organization may decide that it will, as a matter of policy, carry out a freedom for use review:

- before the investment in a technology becomes significant;
- before any technology's commercial exploitation;
- before a bid is submitted to a third party.

Criteria can be developed to help decide whether, and when, such a review will be carried out. Suitable criteria could include:

- the level of financial investment being made;
- the organization's financial dependency on the technology;
- the technology's maturity, that is, whether it has already been used by a number of unrelated organizations;
- whether the technology is clearly a development of a third party's products or services.

These criteria can even be implanted into existing business processes to help decide whether, and when, projects should be subject to a freedom for use review.

Freedom for use review – the process

Figure 17.2 describes the process typically followed to check for third party patents.

It is worth noting that once an organization has been routinely carrying out freedom for use reviews for a number of years it will have established a database of cleared technologies. Assuming these reviews are routinely updated then the work involved in clearing a new project, product or service is generally reduced, as it is only its new components that need to be assessed.

The project, product or service will be split into a number of discrete technical components. Technologies already covered by an up-to-date freedom for use review are disregarded.

For the remaining areas, databases of published patents are searched to identify patents of potential concern. This search will make use of:

- keywords describing the technology;
- the names of relevant companies;
- the names of known third party inventors;
- classification codes* relevant to each element of the project, product or service.

This stage inevitably tends to be iterative, with new search parameters being identified as the search progresses.

A course screening will initially be carried out making use of the patent's title and abstract only. This will discard those patents that clearly have no relevance to the project or service.

A detailed review will then take place of the remaining patents, generally by making reference to the patent's claims. In some instances this may require detailed legal advice and interpretation.

If the exercise identifies any third party patents that will be infringed by a project, product or service, then a number of options must be considered:

- Challenging the patent's validity (if grounds can be found)
- Seeking a licence from the right owner
- Designing around the patent
- Abandon the project, product or service.

The Patent Office gives each patent a classification code according to which technology or business area it addresses.

Figure 17.2   The freedom for use review process

Quality vs cost

One of the difficulties with freedom for use reviews is assessing how much time and effort are warranted in each exercise.

In practice no matter how much time is spent on a freedom for use review it is not possible to be 100 per cent certain that there are no relevant third party patents. Risk is reduced with increased expenditure, but there is clearly a cut-off point beyond which it is not worth incurring further costs.

This cost vs quality decision is evident when considering search parameters. For example, should search terms be combined to reduce the number of patents identified for review (for example, should all competitor's patents be reviewed or just those that have an appropriate classification code?). No search strategy is 100 per cent reliable, and a search based on combining company names, classification codes and technical descriptions increases the chance of an important patent being missed. As a consequence a freedom for use review should ideally involve reviewing competitors' entire patent portfolio. However, in many instances the cost of such an activity is difficult to justify.

Therefore, in all freedom for use reviews there is a need to assess what level of detail (and cost) is appropriate. Some organizations therefore opt for a layer approach; with key differentiating and enabling technologies subject to detailed review, while more peripheral technologies are only subject to a more superficial review.

It is also possible to develop metrics to help guide how detailed or comprehensive any study should be. Such criteria could make use of the following.

1　　The likelihood of unknown third party patents existing.

The following can be used to help indicate how likely it is that unknown third party patents, or other rights, could exist.

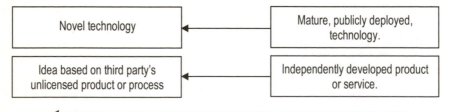

Increasing need for detailed freedom for use review

2   The project's dependency on the technology.

It may be appropriate to undertake a less rigorous review if it is possible for a project to switch to an alternative technology in the event that it was found to be infringing third party rights.

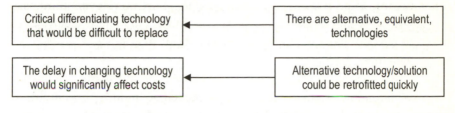

Increasing need for detailed freedom for use review

3   The financial consequences of any infringement.

Clearly there is a relationship between the financial consequences of infringement and the expenditure that can be justified in identifying such a risk.

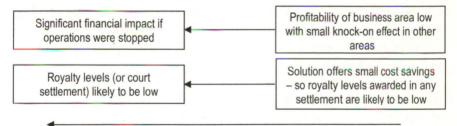

Increasing need for detailed freedom for use review

An organization may also wish to factor in the chances of any infringement being spotted in deciding the appropriate depth of a freedom for use review. However, this is a sensitive area – the courts will look unfavourably on any organization found to be infringing if they have a procedure or practice in which third party rights are only searched for if there is a high chance that infringement will be identified by a third party and action taken.

Timing

Care also needs to be taken when deciding the timing of any freedom for use review activity.

If a review is undertaken early in the development programme then the design may be too fluid and it may not be possible to focus the search, screening and interpretation. Also, if there is a significant chance that the project may be terminated due to commercial or technical reasons then money spent on due diligence will be wasted.

However, it is appropriate to carry out a review before significant expenditure is made by the project, relative to the cost of the freedom for use review. Also, information on third party rights should generally be identified before detailed design begins. Depending on the nature of the project it may therefore be appropriate to complete the freedom for use review either:

- before the final choice of technology is made; or
- before the detailed design starts.

There is also the danger of a freedom for use review for one project discovering problems associated with a technology already deployed. Making a decision on whether to review a technology already deployed, but about to be subject to more open exploitation, is a particularly difficult decision for an organization to make.

Experimental infringement

The UK Patents Act allows experimental work to be undertaken even if it nominally infringes a third party's patents. However, two criteria must be met:

- The work must be purely experimental. There is no definition of "experimental" in the Act; instead, case law must be relied on. As such this book cannot provide definitive advice. However, laboratory-scale experiments will be allowed to examine if, and how, the invention works; also to check whether the technique is appropriate for a generic problem is likely to be allowable. However, instances that are probably not allowed would include demonstrations for potential customers or detailed studies to ascertain how the invention would be used in practice.

- The experiment in question must relate to the patented features. It is not allowed to use a patented technique while carrying out experiments into an unrelated technique or technology.

Damages

There are two basic methods used by the courts to determine the level of damages:

- The profit lost by the intellectual property holder as a result of the infringement.
- Determining a fair share of the profit made by the infringing company, that is, at least a reasonable royalty.

A decision will also need to be made on whether the damages should be based on:

- the actual profit made, or the profit that should have been made;
- the total profit made in the infringing business or the incremental profit resulting from the infringement.

In the final analysis it is difficult, at the outset of a court case, to be certain how the damages will be determined – especially if a jury is involved. This is one reason why most cases of alleged infringement are settled out of court.

Examples:

- In 1985, in the largest ever award arising from a patent-infringement case, a US Federal judge ruled that the Eastman Kodak Company infringed Polaroid Corporation's instant photography patents. Infringement damages to the amount of $873 million were awarded, along with an injunction against further marketing of the infringing camera. However, the case generated uncertainty on the level of damages likely to be awarded in any given case, since it was well below the $12 billion sought by Polaroid and the $1.5 to $2 billion that financial analysts had expected.[1]

---

1   *New York Times,* 13 October 1990.

- In January 2003 the US District Court awarded Igen International damages from a dispute arising from several contracts with Roche Holding, AG. The dispute involved the use of Igen's Origen technology in Roche's Elecsys clinical-testing product line. The jury found contract breaches, and that as a result Igen had the right to terminate its agreement with Roche, and further to gain rights to the Elecsys diagnostic line. The damages were $505 million including punitive damages of $400 million.

- Steelcase Inc paid its rival office furniture manufacturer Haworth Inc $211.5 million for infringing Haworth's patent for prewired office panels used in office cubicles.[2] The invention made it easier to plug computers into most workplace desktops by equipping wall panels for office cubicles with wiring and outlets. The patent dispute arose in 1979 and eventually went to trial in 1985.

- Jerome Lemelson was one of America's most prolific inventors, with nearly 600 patents to his name. He won a total of c.$500 million from over 40 automotive and electronics companies. During the course of his career Lemelson made numerous unsolicited invention submissions while seeking to license his many patents. In some instances these ideas were used by the recipient without seeking a licence agreement.[3]

- Fonar sued Hitachi and General Electric for infringement of its MRI (magnetic resonance imaging) patent. Hitachi settled early in the case, but in 1997 the jury found that General Electric infringed Fonar's patent and awarded damages of $128 million. The first MRI was constructed by its inventor, Dr Raymond Damadian, together with his two post-graduate assistants, almost 20 years earlier. Numerous legal battles were fought against companies such as Siemens, Philips, Toshiba and Hitachi.[4]

Discovery and privileged information

In litigation the court will require the defence to submit a list of documents which relate to the issue being considered. This is an extremely important stage in any action and many cases are won or lost by what is discovered. A

---

2   *Wall Street Journal*, 31 December 1996.
3   *Wall Street Journal*, 16 April 1997.
4   *Business Wire*, October 1997.

solicitor will identify which documents are privileged and can be withheld in their entirety or have sections removed from them. There are three grounds for this withholding:

- It is legally privileged. Privileged information covers communication between legal representatives and clients. It also covers the generation of information requested by the legal advisors – however, this protection is only afforded once litigation is envisaged.
- It is self-incriminating – although this is only a limited right, protecting only civil prosecution.
- There is a public policy issue.

There are limits on what can be requested – it is not a "fishing expedition" by the prosecution looking for unrelated information. The process of discovery – identifying information to be released/requested – is often the most costly element of litigation.

It is possible to get a court to order access to information and for a "raid" to be made. However, this action is normally only taken when there are grounds for believing information may be destroyed. Normally, information is gathered without this action.

Information provided by disenchanted employees is another important route for the prosecution to gain information.

Informing infringers

This is a difficult area – if a threat of action is issued to an alleged infringer, the plaintive may become liable to a counter claim if the basis of that threat proves to be unjustified. This liability exists even if the threat was made in good faith. The wording of letters notifying companies that they may be infringing is a matter that must be considered with great care. A weakly worded letter may be ignored, while a strongly worded one may ultimately result in a counter claim.

Particular care must be taken if information is to be given to those not directly involved in the act of infringement. Letters issued to distributors or other organizations stating that their supplier is infringing should be avoided if possible. In this instance, should the allegations not be upheld, a counter claim is likely, seeking restitution for any damage made to the alleged infringer's business reputation and sales.

INTELLECTUAL PROPERTY RIGHTS

As previously described, intellectual property rights are legal rights, granted by the State, restricting unauthorized use of intellectual property. Under English law[1] infringement of certain intellectual property rights constitutes a criminal offence. Criminal action can therefore be taken against infringers by bodies such as Trading Standards and Customs & Exercise. In addition Civil law provides a framework that enables both individuals and organizations to use litigation to enforce their intellectual property rights through the courts.

There are two ways in which intellectual property rights can be classified. Specifically, according to:

- Whether the rights are granted automatically, or by a legal process involving the registration of the intellectual property with the relevant authorities.
- Whether the rights prevent *use* or whether the protection only prevents *copying* (for example, if a third party produces articles to the same design as your own, then they have only infringed your design rights if they actually copied your designs; if the design was produced independently then infringement has not taken place. However, if a patent exists, then a third party is guilty of infringement with, or without, copying taking place).

Figure A.1 uses this classification system to describe the six principal forms of intellectual property right.

---

1   Although the fundamentals of intellectual property legislation are common across most countries, there is some regional variation. This chapter describes the position under the laws of England.

	Rights granted automatically?	Use or copying prevented?
Patents	no	use
Registered design	no	use
Copyright	yes	copying
Design right	yes	copying
Trademark	yes – but additional rights available	use
Confidentiality undertakings	yes – but additional rights available	in theory just copying

Figure A.1   The six types of intellectual property right

It should also be noted that some "assets" can be simultaneously protected by more than one form of intellectual property right. For instance, a document's text will be protected by copyright, the idea it describes could be protected by a patent, the font will be protected by design right, while the header on the page could be protected by a trademark.

At the most basic level most countries operate similar systems of intellectual property protection. However, at the detailed level, there is considerable variation in both the nature of the rights granted and how the courts interpret these rights.

Figure A.2 summarizes the intellectual property rights that are available to individuals and organizations (apologies to experts at the gross simplifications). These are explored in more detail in the rest of this Appendix.

PATENTS

Patents primarily protect inventions describing processes, products or compositions of matter. Patents give their owner the right to stop others from exploiting, selling, or offering to sell the invention described within the patent:

	Patents	Registered design	Trademark	Copyright	Design right	Obligation of confidence
Scope of protection	Protection is available for processes, products or compositions of matter	Protection is available for the appearance of a device not its functionality	Protection is available for words or symbols (called a device) as used to show the origin of goods or services	Protection is available for the presentation of an idea, whether in the form of reports, music, drawings, paintings, and so on	Protection is afforded to the appearance not the functionality	Protection is available for information received in confidence
Process of winning rights	Rights granted by a complex, long and expensive process of registration	Rights granted by a generally simple and cheap process of registration	Some protection is available automatically; other rights available by a process of registration	Rights granted automatically	Rights granted automatically	There must be an implied or contractual obligation of confidentiality
When does infringement occur	Infringement occurs even without copying	Infringement occurs even without copying	Infringement takes place if the trademark is used to market goods or services in the same market (called class)	Infringement occurs only if copying has taken place	Infringement occurs only if copying has taken place	Information can only be used by the recipient as expressly agreed
Does the granting of rights depend on novelty?	The idea must be new so it cannot have been published prior to registration	In general the design must be new so it cannot have been published prior to registration	The trademark must not already be registered or in use by another organization active in the same class	Protection still exists even if material is released into the public domain	Protection still exists even if material is released into the public domain	Protection only applies to material that is, and remains, confidential in nature
Life of protection	Protection lasts for 20 years, but only if renewal fees are paid	Protection lasts for 25 years	Protection lasts indefinitely, provided the trademark remains in use and renewal fees paid	Protection last for life of author plus 70 years	Protection lasts for 15 years after marketing first occurs or 10 years after manufacture begins	No time limit to rights unless expressly agreed
Comments	In most countries the first to file is entitled to the patent; in the US this is the first to invent		To be registerable a name cannot be a description of the goods or services			It is unwise to rely on implied obligations of confidentiality

Figure A.2 Summary of intellectual property rights

- For a patent to be granted the invention must be novel, capable of industrial application and non-obvious. In most countries there is a process of examination to ensure the invention meets these criteria.
- The need to demonstrate novelty means that the invention must not have been published, or otherwise put into the public domain, before patent protection is sought.
- In most instances a patent will be awarded to the organization or individual who was first to seek a patent – which is not necessarily the first to invent. However, the US have a system where the first to invent is entitled to a patent.
- Patents are territorial – a patent gives its owner the right to stop others producing, using, importing or exporting within the protected territory.
- Once granted, patent protection lasts for a finite period, although it needs to be renewed by paying fees at fixed periods. If a patent is abandoned the rights cannot be reinstated.
- Patenting is expensive: typically an organization will spend between £100 k and £200 k to protect a single invention for the full 20-year term of a patent in around ten countries.
- As part of the patenting process the invention is published. This may be regarded as a disadvantage, and organizations may therefore choose to keep an invention secret rather than seek patent protection.
- Once granted, a patent can still be revoked if it can be shown that the invention was not novel, it is not capable of industrial application, was obvious, or there were deficiencies in the prosecution process (for example, inaccurate information was provided to the Patent Office), and so on.

Note: A patent does not grant its owner, or licensee, the right to perform the activities it describes; as often a patent describes an improvement to a third party's patented idea. The owner of the "improvement patent" cannot practise this improvement without a licence to the "base patent". Patents must therefore be thought of as giving their owner, or licensee, the right to stop others' actions; they do not bestow the right to perform the invention they describe.

Organizations therefore do not patent inventions to preserve the right to carry out the described invention, but to stop others applying it.

REGISTERED DESIGNS

This form of right covers the appearance of a device, but does not extend to cover its functionality. Specifically, the protection is attracted to shape, configuration, patterns and ornamentation. The business sector where this form of protection is most useful is consumer products, where a product's appearance is critical in gaining sales:

- As in the case of patents, this form of protection is not available if there has been disclosure before protection is sought. However, in some territories this restriction only applies if there has been disclosure in the territory where protection is being sought.
- To win legal protection the design must be registered; however, this is a relatively simple and cheap process.
- Protection is again territorial in nature.
- Protection lasts 25 years.

COPYRIGHT AND RELATED RIGHTS

Copyright is critical in certain industries such as publishing, computer software and music:

- Protection is attached to the way an idea is presented, whether in the form of reports, drawings, photographs, paintings, software, music, and so on, not the idea itself (that is, it stops a third party copying a report, but does not protect the ideas within that report).
- The right is granted automatically and does not require registration.
- Infringement occurs only if copying has taken place.
- Protection still exists even if material is released into the public domain.
- Protection generally last for the life of author plus 70 years.

There are two forms of copyright protection:

- Economic rights which prevent acts such as copying and broadcasting.
- Moral rights that help ensure that an author's name is always associated with his or her work and the work's "integrity" is not interfered with.

Reproduction by photocopying, faxing, scanning, and so on are disallowed, but copyright does not prevent the concepts within a document from being extracted and used. The reproduction of all, or a "substantial" part, of the protected material is disallowed. However, there is often uncertainty as to what constitutes a substantial proportion of a protected item. This uncertainty exists because substantiality is an issue of quality, not quantity, and copyright can be infringed even if a relatively small proportion of an asset is copied.

In the case of software, copyright prevents both the unauthorized copying of a program and its adaptation. Both literal and non-literal copying are prevented:

- Literal copying is the simple copying of lines of code.
- Non-literal copying is where the structure or feel of the program is copied.

Databases also have some protection under both copyright and related legislation. This can cover the structure of the database.

DESIGN RIGHTS

Design right is like copyright in that the protection arises automatically when the design is created. As is also the case with copyright, it does not prevent the copying of the ideas or concepts behind the design.

Design right is afforded to the shape or configuration of products. Two-dimensional designs, such as textile or wallpaper designs, are not granted protection, although these qualify for copyright and possibly registered design protection. The protection is not available to "ordinary or well known designs", nor to features which exist to enable one product to be functionally fitted or aesthetically matched.

For the first five years after marketing, design right prevents unauthorized copying; after this period the rights holder must grant licensed rights to anyone requesting such rights.

Unlike copyright, design right is effective only in the United Kingdom.

TRADEMARKS

A trademark can be a word or a symbol (called a device) used to distinguish goods or services:

- A trademark can be registered. However, registration is not always necessary as legislation exists in many countries to protect owners of unregistered trademarks. However, registration does provide additional rights and involves a check to ensure that the trademark is not already in use by a third party.
- A registered trademark must not be a description of the goods being sold.
- The protection is territorial in nature. But unlike other forms of intellectual property right the protection is only granted in particular market sectors (called classes). It is therefore possible for different organizations to use identical trademarks provided their markets do not overlap.
- A registered trademark can be renewed, for a fee, indefinitely. If a trademark is abandoned by failing to pay a fee, then it may be possible to win back the right, but only by starting the registration process again and only if no other organization has claimed the trademark.
- If a registered trademark is not being used it can be revoked, an organization may therefore need to supply proof that a trademark is in use to win, or keep, the trademark.

Three-dimensional devices, the shape of products and style of packaging can all potentially be protected by registration as a trademark. However, a trademark application will only be successful if the shape is an innovative design, unique to your offering, and is not simply a result of the product's function.

There are therefore occasions when it is possible to seek protection either by taking out a registered design, or by filing a trademark. In many instances a registered design will be the preferred option because it is both cheaper and quicker to win. However, if there has been disclosure prior to seeking registration then a registered design will be refused; in this case a trademark will be the only option available.

BREACH OF CONFIDENCE

Breach of confidence provides some protection for material that is confidential. Essentially, legislation provides that confidential information received under an obligation of confidentiality may not be used by the receiving party without permission. However, if the material has been put into the public domain by its owner, or its agents, then it is no longer confidential and is not granted any protection.

An obligation of confidentiality normally arises when two parties enter into a formal agreement under which specified information is released for a specified purpose. In addition there can be an implied duty of confidence created by the transfer of confidential information, even if no formal agreement is in place. However, it is unwise to rely on such implied obligations; instead the transfer of information should normally take place against an enabling agreement.

Further, all employees owe an obligation of confidence to their employers, and consultants owe a duty to their clients. These obligations may be supplemented by employment or other contracts. In the absence of express terms in the contract of employment there is nothing improper about an ex-employee applying his or her "normal skill and knowledge" for a competitor. However, the employee's rights do not extend to the use of trade secrets. Trade secrets can be interpreted as knowledge that, if released, would result in commercial damage to their owner. Unfortunately, there will often be difficulty in clearly defining what knowledge is a trade secret, and what knowledge should be regarded the employee's own skill. Certainly an employee supplementing his or her memory by taking copies of information, which was held in confidence, would normally be regarded as a breach of confidence.

SOFTWARE

The principal protection available to software developers is provided by copyright legislation. This prevents unauthorized adaptation of a programme or the copying of a "substantial" part of it.

Both literal and non-literal copying is prevented:

- Literal copying is the simple copying of lines of code.

- Non-literal copying is where the structure of feel of the programme is copied.

The code itself, the structure of the programme and the functionality of the user interface are granted some protection. However, in practice it may be difficult to show that the structure or feel of a programme has been copied, rather than independently created. If the structure and feel of two programmes in question are similar, and there are clearly many ways in which the programme could have been arranged, then the courts are far more likely to find that copying has taken place.

The basic concepts and idea(s) behind a programme are not protected by copyright, just the expression of that idea. In practice it is often difficult to separate an idea from the expression of that idea, so how the courts will rule is sometimes uncertain. In general the courts will be reluctant to side with an organization that has clearly made unauthorized use of another's work. However, if there is only one way of expressing an idea then it will be difficult for the plaintive to argue that what has been copied is not the idea but the expression of that idea – there is no protection if the appearance or structure is an inevitable consequence of the task being undertaken by the programme.

It should also be noted that preparatory and intermediate works, such as flow charts and specifications, are also protected by copyright.

There would clearly be little doubt how a court would react to a wholesale, unauthorized, copying of an organization's computer code. In other instances where the structure and appearance have been copied there may be a level of uncertainty on how any court would react – the case would inevitably hinge around the facts of the individual case.

In the US, software can be patented if it is novel, non-obvious and produces a "useful, concrete and tangible" result. A similar position exists in Japan.

In Europe, historically, computer programmes "as such" have not been patentable. Patent protection has only been available where computer programmes are incorporated into a machine or processes, and where the resulting system or process is patentable. However, there has been some recent softening of the position and a computer programme, which has a "technical effect" which goes beyond the "normal" physical interactions between the program and the computer on which it is run, may be patentable. Such a technical effect would obviously be present if the computer programme controls a piece of machinery; however, a technical effect has been taken to include the control of computer system resources.

INDEX

If you have found this book useful you may be interested in other titles from Gower

Buying Knowledge:
Effective Acquisition of External Knowledge
Peter Sammons
0 566 08635 2

Leveraging Corporate Knowledge
Edward Truch
0 566 08576 3

Making Knowledge Visible:
Communicating Knowledge Through
Information Products
Elizabeth Orna
0 566 08563 1

Information Risk and Security: Preventing and
Investigating Workplace Computer Crime
Edward Wilding
0 566 08685 9

Information Security and Employee Behaviour:
How to Reduce Risk Through Employee
Education, Training and Awareness
Angus McIlwraith
0 566 08647 6

Information Strategy in Practice
Elizabeth Orna
0 566 08579 8

For more information visit www.gowerpub.com

GOWER

Join our e-mail newsletter

Gower is widely recognized as one of the world's leading publishers on management and business practice. Its programmes range from 1000-page handbooks through practical manuals to popular paperbacks. These cover all the main functions of management: human resource development, sales and marketing, project management, finance, and so on. Gower also produces training videos and activities manuals on a wide range of management skills.

As our list is constantly developing you may find it difficult to keep abreast of new titles. With this in mind we offer a free e-mail news service, approximately once every two months, which provides a brief overview of the most recent titles and links into our catalogue, should you wish to read more or see sample pages.

To sign up to this service, send your request via e-mail to info@gowerpub.com. Please put your e-mail address in the body of the e-mail as confirmation of your agreement to receive information in this way.

GOWER